OLIGOSPERMIA
IN THE LIGHT OF UNANI & MODERN MEDICINE

Shaikh Imtiyaz; S Javed Ali

Title: Oligospermia In the light of Unani & Modern medicine

Authors: Shaikh Imtiyaz; S Javed Ali

Edition: First

Year of Publishing: 2024

Price: 250/-

Publisher: Notion Press, India

Printer: Notion Press, India

ISBN:

AJMAL KHAN TIBBIYA COLLEGE
ALIGARH MUSLIM UNIVERSITY, ALIGARH - 202002

اجمل خان طبیہ کالج، علی گڑھ مسلم یونیورسٹی، علی گڑھ

अजमल ख़ॉं तिब्बिया कॉलेज, अलीगढ़ मुस्लिम विश्वविद्यालय, अलीगढ़

PRINCIPAL / پرنسپل / प्रधानाचार्य

Ref. No. ....   Dated ....

Foreword

It brings me great pleasure to contribute a foreword for the book entitled *Oligospermia In the Light of Unani and Modern Medicine*, authored by my dear student, *Dr. S Javed Ali*, Assistant Professor, Department of Moalejat, Ajmal Khan Tibbiya College, AMU, Aligarh; alongside *Dr. Shaikh Imtiyaz*, Assistant Professor, Department of Moalejat, MTCH, Mansoora, Malegaon. This collaborative effort represents an outstanding contribution to a topic that is often overlooked in medical literature. Through their meticulous research and dedication, the authors have created a novel and comprehensive resource.

Infertility, defined as the inability of a couple to conceive after one year of regular, unprotected intercourse, is a deeply personal and challenging issue for many. It affects a significant percentage of couples worldwide, with male factor infertility accounting for a substantial portion of cases. Oligospermia, characterized by low sperm count, is a primary contributor to male infertility. Drawing upon both Unani and modern medical perspectives, this book delves into the complexities of oligospermia, offering insights into its etiology, diagnosis, and treatment options.

The authors have provided a thorough exploration of the historical context of fertility, infertility, and the evolving landscape of sexual medicine. They meticulously examine the various dimensions of oligospermia, bridging the gap between traditional Unani practices and contemporary medical advancements. From the historical background to the latest treatment modalities, this book offers a comprehensive overview of the subject.

I commend the authors for their meticulous planning and lucid presentation of the material, making it accessible to students, clinicians, and researchers alike. Their dedication to addressing this important medical issue is evident throughout the pages of this book. I have no doubt that their efforts will have a significant impact on the field of reproductive medicine.

In closing, I extend my heartfelt congratulations to Dr. S Javed Ali and Dr. Shaikh Imtiyaz for their commendable achievement. May this book serve as a valuable resource for all who seek understanding and guidance in the realm of oligospermia. Let us embrace their work with open minds and hearts, recognizing its potential to improve the lives of countless individuals and families affected by infertility.

Furthermore, it is worth noting the rich heritage of Unani medicine in providing holistic care for various diseases, including infertility. This book stands out for its inclusion of both single and compound Unani drugs for the treatment of oligospermia, offering a comprehensive approach rooted in centuries of traditional wisdom. With deep introductions and historical insights, the authors provide readers with a profound understanding of Unani medicine's approach to reproductive health. As we celebrate the publication of this important book, let us also acknowledge the tireless efforts of healthcare professionals and institutions like Ajmal Khan Tibbiy College Hospital in advancing the field of Unani medicine and improving healthcare outcomes for all.

Badrudduja

(Prof. Badrudduja Khan)
Principal

Preface

Oligospermia (Qilatte Haiwane Manwiya) is one of the most common causes of male infertility. Despite numerous advances in the management of male infertility, this issue has not been satisfactorily resolved. Various defects in spermatozoa found on semen analysis contribute to male infertility, including an inadequate number of spermatozoa in semen and the failure of spermatozoa to move with adequate power and speed toward their target. This condition directly correlates with male infertility, defined as the failure of a couple to achieve conception after one year of regular unprotected intercourse. It poses a distressing problem for 10-15%

of the population, with its incidence steadily increasing over the years. Recent studies have indicated a decrease in sperm densily over the past fifty years, further highlighting the urgency of addressing this issue. While infertility affects both men and women, male factor infertility accounts for approximately 30-40% of cases. Eminent Unani physicians have been treating this problem since time immemorial, aiming not only to improve the number of spermatozoa but also to address other defects associated with them. Almost every Unani treatise extensively discusses Qilatte Haiwune Manwiya, covering its causes, pathology, pathogenesis, clinical presentation, line of treatment, and a vast array of treatment options.

This book aims to encompass all available literature on oligospermia in both Unani and modern systems of medicine. It is divided into several chapters, covering the historical background of infertility and oligospermia in detail. Additionally, causes, pathogenesis, investigations, and treatment options are thoroughly discussed. Towards the end, research and clinical trials of Unani medicines regarding oligospermia are also examined.

The language of the book is simple and easily understandable. Each topic is explained in a straightforward manner, broken down into easily memorable short points. This book will prove helpful for clinicians, postgraduate scholars, and teachers alike.

We also acknowledge the valuable contributions of some of our students and staff, especially Ms. Ummay Kulsum and Mr. Sharjeel ur Rahman (Naved), who provided insightful perspectives and assistance during the preparation of this book.

We hope that this book will be widely read and accepted among the teachers and student community of Unani medicine.

Authors

CONTENT

i.	Foreword	iii
ii.	Preface	iv
1.	INTRODUCTION	1
2.	HISTORICAL BACKGROUND	8
3.	DEFINITION OF OLIGOSPERMIA	19
4.	MANI IN UNANI MEDICINE	22
5.	ANATOMY OF MALE REPRODUCTIVE ORGANS	25
6.	TAWLEED MADDAE MANIWIYA	34
7.	SPERMATOGENESIS	37
8.	HORMONES AFFECTING SPERMATOGENESIS	41
9.	SPERMATOZOA	43
10.	EPIDEMIOLOGY OF OLIGOSPERMIA	44
11.	ETIOLOGY	45
12.	DIAGNOSIS	56
13.	MANAGEMENT OF OLIGOSPERMIA	62
14.	USOOLE ILAJ WA ILAJ	66
15.	COMMONLY USED MUFRAD ADVIA	69
16.	COMMONLY USED MURAKKAB ADVIA	70

17.	SCIENTIFIC PROVEN SINGLE DRUGS FOR OLIGOSPERMIA	71
18.	SCIENTIFIC PROVEN COMPOUND DRUGS FOR OLIGOSPERMIA	145
19.	APHRODISIACS IN UNANI MEDICINE	155
20.	IMPORTANCE OF SEXUAL INTERCOURSE (JIMA) ACCORDING TO USM	162
21.	BIBLIOGRAPHY	172

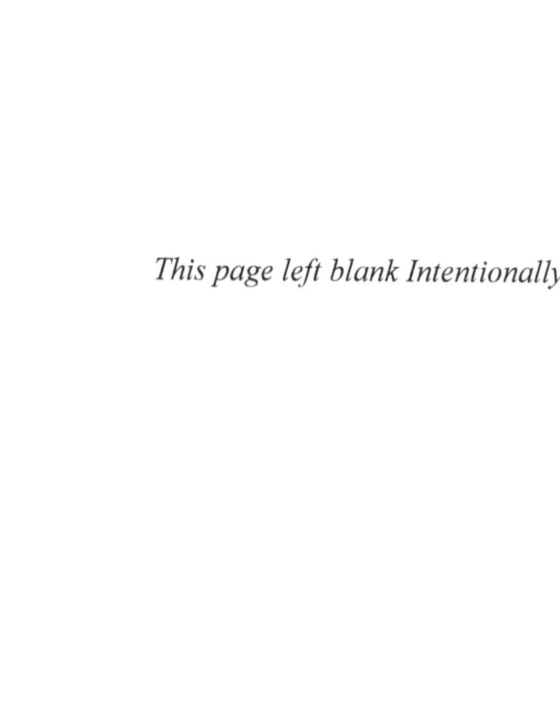

This page left blank Intentionally

INTRODUCTION

Oligospermia (*Qillate haiwane manwiya*) is one of the most common afflictions of male reproductive system. It is a condition in which the sperm count is decreased to less than 15 million/ml of semen. However, some investigators considered sperm count less than 20 million/ml also as oligospermia. The important causes include varicocoele, cryptorchidism, klinefelter's syndrome, damaged testes due to trauma or infections (tuberculosis, syphilis, mumps), neoplasm of testes, kidney and liver diseases, smoking, alcoholism, wearing tight under wear, working at high temperature places like welding, dyeing, blast furnace, cement and steel factories etc. These factors are directly associated with male infertility and other related sexual dysfunctions. Infertility is defined as the failure of a couple to achieve conception after one year of regular unprotected intercourse. Infertility is a distressing problem for 10-15% of the population, with the incidence increasing over the years. However it affects both men and women, but male factor contributes to about 30-40% cases of infertility. In many couples both male and female factor coincide. In case of a single factor, the fertile partner may compensate for the less fertile partner.

The incidence of infertility is increasing globally. A recent study has indicated that there is a decrease in sperm density over a period of past fifty years. The prevalence of oligospermia is highest in sub-Saharan Africa (infertility belt). Despite of remarkable advancement in pharmacotherapy, infertility continues to raise significant economic and personal burden to the society. It may be subdivided into primary and secondary infertility. Primary infertility exists when a woman has never been pregnant. Secondary infertility occurs when a woman has a history of one or more previous pregnancies. Infertility is one of the most tragic of all marital problems. Male infertility, with its clinical and psychosocial implications, poses a significant challenge to the physicians and to the society as a whole. It may be due to an inadequate number of spermatozoa in the semen (oligospermia), the failure of the spermatozoa to move with sufficient vigour towards their goal (aesthenospermia) or that they are deficient in other respects. Among various pathologies afflicting humans, infertility has a special place. It usually does not result in a physical morbidity, pain, limitation of activity or longevity. However, its impact on the psychological and social wellbeing of not only the index patient but also his or her partner makes it a major concern for health professionals. People with infertility face a multitude of stressful experiences and decisions. The financial costs, frequent doctor appointments, treatment decisions, painful and sometimes embarrassing procedures and the month-to-month emotional roller coaster impact individuals experiencing infertility.

In Unani system of medicine, most of Unani scholars particularly Ibn Sina (980-1037 AD), Zakaria Razi (865-925 AD), Ismail Jurjani (1110 AD) and Rabban Tabri (810-895 AD) have elaborately discussed sexual diseases in their respective lexicons. They have mentioned the causes, symptoms, complications, treatment and management of various sexual diseases in their treatises under the caption of *Zoafe bah*. In fact, *Zoafe bah* is a broad term which encompasses various sexual disease entities like *Istirkhae Qazeeb*, *Surate Inzaal* and *Qillate Mani* etc. The concept of *Qillate Mani* (*Qillat*- less, *Mani*-semen) can be correlated with the concept of oligospermia (Oligo-less, spermia-spermatozoa). The literal meaning of oligospermia is *Qillate haiwane manwiya*. The important causes of *Qillate mani* are *kasrate istifragh*, excessive use of *mudirrat*, *sue mizaj* of *alaate mani*, excessive use of drugs like *afyoon* (opium) and *bhang* and excessive riding etc.

According to Unani concept, human body is composed of seven essential factors that are *arkan* (elements), *mizaj* (temperament), *akhlat* (humours), *aaza* (organs), *arwah* (pneuma), *quwa* (faculties) and *afaal* (functions). There are three major *Quwa* viz *Quwwate Nafsaniya*, *Quwwate Haiwaniya* and *Quwwate Tabi'ya*. These *Quwa* are natural and specialized powers which are responsible for the performance of specific bodily functions. *Quwwate Tabi'ya* is concerned with *Taghzia* (nutrition) and *Namu wa Tawleed* (growth and reproduction), *Jigar* (liver) is considered as *Uzwe Raees* (vital organ) of this *Quwwat*. *Quwwate Haiwaniya* is concerned with *Tadbeer of Rooh*, which brings life to the part it supplies. *Qalb* (heart) is *Uzwe Raees* of this faculty. *Quwwat Nafsaniya* is concerned with sensory and motor functions. The *Uzwe Raees* for this faculty is *Dimagh* (brain).

Quwwate Tanasuliyah (reproductive faculty) is a type of *Quwate Tabi'ya* which controls propagation and preservation of the species to replace what is lost through the death of its members. It is responsible for the production of *Mani* (semen) i.e. sperm and ovum; for all sexual functions and formation of the *Janeen* (foetus) in the uterus. Reproduction is an important part of life without which the propagation of that particular species will be ceased.

The principle of treatment in Unani system of medicine is based on the concept of organ protection, strengthening and maintenance of the *Quwa* at their equilibrium (*etedal*). The faculties at their equilibrium are poised inherently to maintain the normal function of that organ or system. It has been mentioned that each organ is bestowed with special *Quwat* for its optimal functioning. *Unsiyaen* are the *azae raesa* for *Quwwate Tanasuliya*. In case of derangement of function (*zoaf*) of any organ, the drugs enhancing its power (*muqawwi advia*) are advocated. This is the reason why in Unani system of medicine, for every organ and system, a group of tonic drugs (*muqawwi advia*) have been proposed that safe guard its larger interest and bring it near to equilibrium, if some derangement in its structure or function takes place. Therefore, most of the sexual diseases are being treated on the basis of concept of *Taqwiyate aaza*.

There is a treasure of single and compound Unani drugs which are used for male sexual weakness (*Zoafe bah*) and infertility.The *mufrad advia* useful in *Qillate mani* are *Salab misri, Khurma, Singhara, Taranjabeen, Tukhme shaljam, Kharkhsak, Nakhud siyah, Todri, Funduq, Maghze chilghoza, Pyaz kham, Bahman safed* etc. These drugs possess properties like *Muqqawie bah, Muwallide mani, Mughallize mani, Musammine badan* etc, and act by virtue of potentiating the action of *Quwwate Tanasuliya* and thereby acts as *Muwallide mani.*

HISTORICAL BACKGROUND

As it is evident from carvings and cave drawings that the stone-age people had some knowledge of anatomy and the reproductive process, but the first detailed information comes from Egyptian Papyrus, which describes many gynaecological complaints and recipes to increase fertility. Various passages in the Bible confirm the interest of ancient Hebrews in the fertility process, and they were aware that conception was possible 7 days after the cessation of menses.

It was the Greeks who first defined the human form in sculpture and paintings. Both Buqrat (Hippocrates) and Arastu (Aristotle) were aware of the external and internal reproductive organs, although knowledge of the latter was based mainly on observation and dissection of animals. Buqrat (460-377 BC) was the first to elaborate the anatomical and physiological aspect of testes. He recorded that intercourse was necessary for pregnancy to occur. He believed that semen and menstrual blood mixed in the uterus to form a fetus.

Andreas Vesalius (1514-1564 AD) from the University of Padua, published his *De Humani Corporis Fabrica*. This was the first anatomical book based on human dissection by the author with illustrations by Jan Stephan van Kalkar.

In 1621 AD, Fabricius believed that the fertilizing principle of semen was an emanation which was called the *Aura Seminalis*. Thirty years later Harvey developed this thinking further, as 'after intercourse there is nothing more to be found in the uterus than was there before the act'. He theorized that uterus was brought to a stage of ripeness by copulation. It could then proceed to a conception state through the stimulus of the *aura seminalis*, and apparently no physical agent took any part in the process.

The physiology of erection was founded on the work of Muller in 1838 and also on the studies of Eckhard and other.

Advances in the investigation and treatment of infertility gained impetus from scientific research in the fields of embryology, physiology gynaecological endocrinology, culdoscopy, laparoscopy, ultrasound and laboratory techniques and management of infertility. Eventually in the 1980s the assisted conception technologies became available.

The important historical events of reproduction, fertility and infertility are summarized below.

Buqrat (460-377 BC) gave the complete anatomical and physiological description of testes.

Jalinoos (131-201 AD) taught that there was a mixing of male and female semen from the ovaries, with the formation of a conception.

Rabban Tabri (810-895 AD) mentioned the process of gestational development of fetus in his book *Firdausul Hikmat* (The Paradise of Wisdom).

Zakariya Razi (865- 925 AD) in *Kitabul Mansuri* mentioned the anatomy of testes, and in *Kitabul*

Havi mentioned various sexual disorders along with their management.

Ali Ibn Abbas Majoosi (930- 999AD) in his book *Kamilus Sina'ah* described the diseases of male and female reproductive system, and discussed about their treatment in detail.

Ibn Sina (980-1037 AD) gave the complete description of anatomy and physiology of male reproductive system along with comprehensive discussion of different ailments of male reproduction in his treatise *Alqanoon fit Tib* (The Cannon of medicine). He also put forth the concept of *Quwa* (faculties) governing the process of reproduction.

Ismail Jurjani (1110 AD) in his book *Zakhira khwarzam Shahi* explained the process of formation of semen, he also explored different sexual diseases.

Ibn Rushd (1126-1198 AD) in his book *Kitabul Kulliyat* explained in brief the anatomy of male and female genitals. He also mentioned various aphrodisiac drugs.

Hakim Azam Khan (1315 AD) in his book *Aksire Azam* gave the complete description of various diseases of male and female reproductive system.

1678 AD: Van Leeuwenhoek first described spermatozoa in semen.

1810 AD: Rudolph von Koelleker demonstrated that sperm originated in the testes.

1843 AD: Barry observed fertilization of the rabbit egg.

1865 AD: Franz Schweiger-Scidel showed that sperm cells posses both a nucleus and cytoplasm.

1941 AD: Mac Cleod and Hotchkiss showed that excess heat adversely affected spermatogenesis.

1944 AD: Hotchkiss noted, that approximately 300 million spermatozoa deposited in the vagina, only one meets the ovum in the upper portion of the fallopian tube.

1948 AD: Harrison and Weiner showed that the temperature in the testes is lower than that in the interior of the animal.

1952 AD: Le Blond and Cleromont defined the stages of cycle of development of sperm.

1963 AD: Barer et al noted that while most cells contain approximately 70% water, sperm contain only about 50 %.

1955 AD: Harvey and Jackson discovered that the first part of the ejaculate contains approximately 80 % of the sperm.

1963 AD: Clermont outlined the development of the spermatozoa in man.

1970 AD: Rowley et al estimated that it takes twelve days from time of release in the seminiferous tubules to ejaculation.

1973 AD: Settlage et al found spermatozoa in the fallopian tube within 5 minute of insemination.

1976 AD: Farbas and Rosens demonstrated decreased sperm production in chronic alcohol intake.

1981 AD: Evans at al found incidence of increased sperm abnormalities in smokers.

Semen analysis

1931 AD: Moench and Holt analyzed sperm morphology.

1941 AD: Hotchkiss reviewed factors in stability and variability of semen specimen.

1948 AD: Mann found that sperm density in ejaculates fell as a consequence of repeated ejaculations over a short time.

1951 AD: MacLeod and Gold evaluated semen and found that when the sperm count and motility were satisfactory, morphology was usually normal.

1954 AD: Frank et al found that the presence of more than one million immature forms per ml was associated with a bad prognosis.

1963 AD: Rutherford et al, evaluated semen quality and its relationship to normal unplanned pregnancy.

1965 AD: Murphy and Torrano reported pregnancies in partner of male whose sperm count was as low as one million.

1975 AD: Eliasson endeavored to standardize seminal fluid analysis.

1980 AD: Makler developed a new technique for human sperm motility determination by using microcomputer.

Counts and fertility

1951 AD: MacLeod and Gold showed that there is increased incidence of infertility in patients with sperm count less than 20 million.

1971 AD: The American fertility society indicated that a sperm concentration of 40 million per ml was the lower limit of normal.

1979 AD: Schwartz et al found that for each day of abstinence there was a increased sperm count of 13 million and increased volume of 0.4 ml.

Special tests in the male

1950 AD: Howard et al detailed their experience of testicular biopsy in cases of semen deficiency.

1951 AD: Landau and Loughead discovered that fructose levels correlate positively with androgen levels.

1966 AD: Amelar found that it was rare for oligospermic men to have obstructive lesions.

1973 AD: Phadke et al found that fructose production varied inversely with sperm count.

1976 AD: Yanagimachi et al reported a test in which the ability of human sperm to penetrate zona-free hamster eggs was assessed.

Artificial insemination by donor and husband

3rd C. AD: Artificial insemination was mention in the Babylonian Talmud. It was also felt possible that a woman could conceive as a result of bathing in water into which a man had ejaculated. Women were advised against lying on bed sheets recently vacated by a man other than their husband, in case the man had deposited semen in the bedding and the woman became pregnant.

14th C. AD: Arabs used artificial insemination with horses.

15th C. AD: Fish eggs were artificially impregnated.

1764 AD: Ludwick Jacobi is said to have performed the first successful experiments with artificial impregnation of fish.

1785 AD: John Hunter used artificial insemination in a woman which resulted in the birth of a child.

1868 AD: Marion Sims reported successful artificial insemination by husband in the USA.

1884 AD: Pancoast performed the first successful donor insemination in America.

1972 AD: Jacobs et al indicated that the risk of detecting a serious abnormal autosomal constitution in a phenotypically normal donor was in the order of 3.3 per 1000.

1986 AD: The American fertility society published guidelines for donor screening in a donor insemination programme.

1990 AD: Taymor reviewed results of donor insemination from the literature and found pregnancy rates of 4-56%.

OLIGOSPERMIA (*QILLATE HAIWANE MANWIYA*)

Definition

In classical Unani literature *Qillate Mani* is described under the caption of *Zoafe bah* while, the literal meaning of *Qillate haiwane manwiya* is Oligospermia, a term used in conventional medicine. Oligospermia is a condition where sperm count is less than 20 million/ml of semen.

In the Unani doctrine it is mentioned that for the existence of life of an individual there are three important *Quwa* (faculties) viz *Quwae-Nafsaniya* (psychic or mental faculty), *Quwae-Haiwaniya* (vital faculty) and *Quwae-Tabi'ya* (natural faculty). While for the maintenance of species there is one more *Quwat* namely *Quwae Tanasuliyah* (reproductive faculty) which is a type of *Quwate Tabi'ya* acting on the *ghiza* (food) for the preservation of species. This faculty controls propagation and preservation of a race to replace what is lost due to death of its members, through the production of *mani* (semen) i.e. sperm and ovum; for all sexual functions and formation of the *Janeen* (fetus) in the uterus.

Quwae Tanasuliyah is of two kinds.

1. *Quwate Muwwallidah* (Generative power)

2. *Quwate Musawwirah* (Formative power)

1. *Quwate Muwwallidah*

It is that *Quwat* which separates the essence of *mani* (i.e. sperm or ovum) from *imshaje badan* (compounds of the body) inside the gonads and allows each of its part to become a particular organ. Ibn Sina (980-1037 AD) divided *Quwate Mawwallidah* into two types, one is that which generates *mani* in the male and female, and the other one is that which gives different combinations to different potentialities of the *mani* (sperm and ovum), according to future organs. This *quwat* is also called as *quwate mugayyirah'ula* (Primary transformative power).

Thus, this *quwat* controls *Tauleede haiwane manwiya* (spermatogenesis) in males and *Tauleede baiziyah* (oogenesis), *Amale-Baar awari* (ovulation) and also the process of *Tamas* (menstruation) in females, with the help of different *Raseelat / Akhlate Muharrikah* (hormones) etc. This *Quwat* also determines the different potentialities (genes) and their arrangement in the chromosomes of the sperm and ovum to transfer the hereditary characters of the parents to the offspring; and the type of chromosomes are also determined by it to determine the sex of the offspring.

2) *Quwate Musawwirah*

This *quwat* gives the particular shape to each part of *mani* which is required by that particular species to whom it belongs, or any other shape close to that individual. Giving of shape means it produces lines in the organs, forms cavities and depressions and performs other functions. Ibn Sina says, *Quwate Musawwirah* is that whereby, subject to the grace of Allah, delineation and configuration of the organs is produced with all their cavities, foramina, positions and relations to one another, their smoothness or roughness and so on all being controlled up to the final limits of their natural dimension

MANI (SEMEN) IN UNANI MEDCINE

Mani is whitish viscous fluid with specific odour similar to *talae khurma* (*tari*). It is composed of two parts ie *Manie khas* (*Haiwane manvi*/ Spermatozoa) and secretions which come from seminal vesicle, prostate and *gudade mukhatiya* (mucous glands).

Ibn Sina stated that production of *mani* takes place in *Unsiyaeen. Mani* is formed from that fluid (*rutubat*) which comes in the gonads through blood vessels supplying them. He further added that *mani* is a *fuzla* (waste product) of *hazame chaharum* (fourth stage of metabolism) i.e. *hazame uzwi*, it is produced by extremely *latif* and *pukhta khoon*.

According to Jalinoos (131-201 AD) for male and female there are two types of *zara* / *tukhm* (ie sperm and ovum).

Ismail Jurjani (1110 AD) in his book *Zakhira khwarzam Shahi* wrote that *mani* is a *fuzla* of *hazame chaharum*. It percolates from those vessels which nourishes the gonads, and it is from the group of *rutubate ghariziya qaribul ahd bil ineqad* (a fluid which is about to condense).

Zakariya Razi (865- 925 AD) in his treatise *Kitabul Mansuri* narrates that two canaliculi coming out of peritoneum further divide into two branches which makes inner part of scrotum; scrotum has two *baiza* surrounded by many vessels which further makes many lobules having whitish *lahame gudadi* (glandular muscles).These glandular muscles convert blood into whitish substance which on further *nuzj* in the *Unsiyaeen* gets converted into *mani*.

Semen is composed of the sperm and fluid from the vas deferens, the seminal vesicles, and the prostate gland, and small amounts from the mucous glands especially the bulbourethral glands. The average pH of the semen is about 7.5 (Seven and half). The prostatic fluid gives the semen a milky appearance and fluid from the seminal vesicles and mucous glands gives the semen a mucoid consistency.

Although sperm can live for many weeks in the male genital ducts, once they are ejaculated in the semen, their maximal life span is only 24 to 48 hours at body temperature. At lowered temperatures, however, semen can be stored for several weeks and when frozen at temperatures below -100°C sperm have been preserved for years.

ANATOMY OF MALE REPRODUCTIVE ORGANS

The structures of the male reproductive system can be categorized on a functional basis as follows.

Primary sex organs

The primary sex organs are called gonads specifically, the testes in the male. They produce the spermatozoa and secrete sex hormones (androgens) which at the appropriate times and in sufficient quantities develop secondary sex organs and the expression of secondary sex characteristics.

Secondary sex organs

These structures are essential for transport of spermatozoa. They include epididymis, ductus deferens, ejaculatory ducts, urethra, seminal vesicles, prostate, bulbourethral glands and penis. Scrotum is a pouch of skin that encloses and protects testes.

***Keesae Baiza* (Scrotum)**

It is suspended immediately behind the base of the penis. The functions of the scrotum are to support and protect the testes and to regulate their position relative to the pelvic region of the body. The soft textured skin of the scrotum is covered with sparse hair in mature males and is darker in colour than most of the other skin of the body. It also contains numerous sebaceous glands. The temperature of the testes is maintained at about 35° C (95° F) or about 3.6 ° F below normal body temperature by the contraction or relaxation of the scrotal muscles (dartos). This temperature is optimal for the production and storage of spermatozoa.

***Khusiyataeen / Unsiyaeen* (Testes)**

Unsiyaeen are the paired hollow organs. It is the place where production of *Mani* takes place. Each *Baiza* (testicle) is made up of *lahame abyaz* (white flesh) resembling that of breast. Right *Baiza* is stronger (*Qawi*) than the left one. Blood coming for the nourishment of *Unsiyaeen* is quite *pukhta, pakiza wa saaf.*

The testes are male gonads which produce sperm and also the male sex hormones. They lie outside the abdominal cavity within the scrotum. Each testicle measuring about 5 cm long and 2.5 cm in diameter, having weight of 10-15 grams. A serous membrane called the tunica vaginalis, which is derived from the peritoneum and formed during the descent of the testes, partially covers the testes. Internal to the tunica vaginalis is a white fibrous capsule composed of dense irregular connective tissue, the tunica albuginea, it extends inward, forming septa that divide the testis into a series of internal compartments called lobules. Each of the 200-300 lobules contains one to three tightly coiled tubules, the seminiferous tubules, where sperm are produced. The process by which the seminiferous tubules of the testes produce sperm is called spermatogenesis. The seminiferous tubules contain two types of cells: spermatogenic cells and Sertoli cells, which have several functions in supporting spermatogenesis. In the spaces between adjacent seminiferous tubules are clusters of cells called Leydig (interstitial) cells. These cells secrete testosterone, the most prevalent androgen which is responsible for the development of masculine characteristics.

Spermatic Ducts

The spermatic ducts store the spermatozoa and transport them from the testes to urethra. The accessory reproductive glands provide additives to the spermatozoa in the formation of semen.

Aghdeedoose (Epididymis)

It is an elongated organ attached to the posterior surface of the testis. The uncoiled epididymis will measure 5.5 m. The highly coiled, tubular tail portion contains spermatozoa in their final stages of maturation. The upper expanded portion is the head, and the tapering middle section is the body. The tail is continuous with the beginning portion of the ductus deferens; both store spermatozoa to be discharged during ejaculation.

Majrae Mani (Ductus Deferens)

It is a fibro muscular tube about 45 cm long and 2.5 mm thick that conveys spermatozoa from the epididymis to the ejaculatory duct. It exits the scrotum by ascending along the posterior border of the testis. From here, it penetrates the inguinal canal, enters the pelvic cavity, and passes to the side of the urinary bladder on the medial side of the ureter. The ampulla of the ductus deferens is the terminal portion that joins the ejaculatory duct. Much of the ductus deferens is located within a structure known as the spermatic cord.

Accessory Reproductive Glands

These include seminal vesicles, prostate and bulbourethral glands. The contents of seminal vesicles and prostate mixed with the spermatozoa during ejaculation to form semen. The fluid from the bulbourethral glands is leased in response to sexual stimulation prior to ejaculation.

Seminal Vesicles

The paired seminal vesicles, each about 5 cm long, are convoluted club-shaped glands lying at the base of the urinary bladder, in front of the rectum. They secrete a sticky, slightly alkaline, yellowish substance that contributes to the motility and viability of spermatozoa. The secretion from the seminal vesicles contains a variety of nutrients, including fructose, that provide an energy source for the spermatozoa. It also contains citric acid, coagulation proteins, and prostaglandins. The discharge from the seminal vesicles makes up about 60% of the volume of semen.

Gudae mazi (Prostate)

The size and shape of the prostate gland is as chestnut. It is about 4 cm wide and 3 cm thick and lies just below the urinary bladder where it surrounds the first part of the urethra. The thin, milky-coloured prostatic secretion assists sperm cell motility as a liquefying agent, and its alkaline nature protects the sperm in their passage through the acidic environment of the female vagina. The prostate also secretes the enzyme acid phosphatase, which is often measured clinically to assess prostate function. The discharge from the prostate makes up about 40% of the volume of the semen.

Bulbourethral Glands

They are paired pea-sized glands, located below the prostate. Each one is about 1 cm in diameter and drains by a 2.5cm long duct into urethra. On sexual arousal and prior to ejaculation, they are stimulated to secrete a mucoid substance that coats the lining of the urethra to neutralize the pH of the urine residue. It also lubricates the tip of the penis in preparation for coitus.

Majrae baol/Naiza (Urethra)

The urethra of the male serves as a common tube for both the urinary and reproductive systems. It is about 20 cm long, and S-shaped because of the shape of the penis. It is divided into three regions viz prostatic urethra 2.5 cm, membranous urethra 0.5 cm and penile urethra 15 cm long.

Qazeeb (Penis)

Qazeeb, the male *uzwe taanasul* (copulatory organ) is an *uzwe murakkab*. It is composed of *rebat*, muscles, nerves and blood vessels. In the *jirm* (substance) of *Qazeeb* there are many *tajaveef* (cavities) and a network of arteries. On stimulation these *tajaveef* gets filled with blood and *reeh* (air) causing erection of the organ. Root of the *Qazeeb* is attached to pelvis. There are three *majari* in the *Qazeeb* one is for urine, second for *mani* and third for *wadi*. The nerves supplying to penis emerge from sacral vertebrae. Ibn Sina states that the power of erection comes from *Qalb* (heart), the power of sense from *Dimagh wa nukha* (brain and spinal cord) while *shahwat* comes from *Jigar* (liver). Buqrat says that using the organ (penis) makes it *qawi* while leaving it useless results in *zoaf* (weakness).

The penis contains urethra and is a passageway for the ejaculation of semen and the excretion of urine. It is cylindrical in shape and consists of a body, glans penis, and a root. The body of the penis is composed of three cylindrical masses of tissue; each one is surrounded by fibrous tissue called the tunica albuginea. The two dorso-lateral masses are called the corpora cavernosa penis. The smaller mid ventral mass, the corpus spongiosum penis, contains the spongy urethra and keeps it open during ejaculation. Skin and a subcutaneous layer enclose all three masses, which consist of erectile tissue. Erectile tissue is composed of numerous blood sinuses lined by endothelial cells and surrounded by smooth muscle and elastic connective tissue. The distal end of the corpus spongiosum penis is a slightly enlarged, acorn-shaped region called the glans penis; its margin is known as corona. The distal urethra enlarges within the glans penis and forms a terminal slit like opening, the external urethral orifice. Covering the glans in an uncircumcised penis is the loosely fitting prepuce or foreskin.

TAULEEDE MADDAE MANWIYAH

Ibn Sina in his world renowned treatise *Al Qanoon fit tibb* (The Canon of medicine) states that *Unsiyaeen* (gonads) are a pair of *aazae raeesa* (vital organs) where the production of *mani* takes place. *Mani* is formed from that fluid (*rutubat*) which comes into the gonads through blood vessels supplying them. He adds that *mani* is *fuzla* (waste product) of *hazame chaharum* (fourth stage of metabolism) ie *hazame uzwi*, it is produced by extremely *latif* and *pukhta khoon*.

The *sababe maddi* for *mani* is that part of *ghiza* which has completed *hazame suwwam* and enter in the *hazame chaharum* and is near to condense.

Ismail Ahmed Hasan Jurjani states that the *madda* of *mani* is that *rutubat* which percolates from those vessels which nourishes the gonads, and it is from the group of *rutubate ghariziya qaribul ahd bil ineqad* (a fluid which is about to condense).

As per Unani classic, every individual is endowed with specific *mizaj* (Temperament). Accordingly the characteristics of *mani* and associated symptoms are different for each *mizaj*.

Mizaje Haar

Veins of penis and testes will be prominent, rapidly growing dark and thick pubic hairs, increased libido.

Mizaje Barid

Veins of penis and testes will not prominent, slowly growing thin pubic hairs and low libido.

Mizaje Ratab

Mani will be *raqiq* in consistency and excessive in quantity, low libido and poor erection.

Mizaje Yabis

Mani will be *ghaliz* in consistency and *qalil* in quantity, increased libido and good erection.

Mizaje Haar Yabis

Increased libido, rapidly growing dark and thick pubic hairs, fertility will be more.

Mizaje Haar Ratab

Excessive *mani*, slowly growing pubic hairs, increased libido and premature ejaculation.

Mizaje Barid Ratab

Minimum pubic hairs, diminished libido, reduced fertility and *riqqate mani*.

Mizaje Barid Yabis

Qillate mani and diminished libido

SPERMATOGENESIS

The process of formation of mature spermatozoa is termed as Spermatogenesis. It occurs in the seminiferous tubules during reproductive age as the result of stimulation by anterior pituitary gonadotropic hormones. It begins at an average age of 13 years and continues throughout life but decreasing markedly in old age. In humans takes 65-75 days to complete the process of spermatogenesis. It begins with the spermatogonia, which contain the diploid (2n) number of chromosomes. Spermatogonia are types of stem cells; when they undergo mitosis, some spermatogonia remain near the basement membrane of the seminiferous tubule in an undifferentiated state to serve as a reservoir of cells for future cell division and subsequent sperm production. The rest of the spermatogonia lose contact with the basement membrane, squeeze through the tight junctions of the blood-testis barrier, undergo developmental changes, and differentiate into primary spermatocytes. Primary spermatocytes, like spermatogonia, are diploid (2n); that is they have 46 chromosomes. Shortly after formation each primary spermatocyte replicates its DNA and then meiosis begins. In meiosis I, homologous pairs of chromosomes line up at the metaphase plate, and crossing-over occurs. Then, the meiotic spindle pulls one (duplicated) chromosome of each pair to an opposite pole of the dividing cell. The two cells formed by meiosis I are called secondary spermatocytes. Each secondary spermatocyte has 23 chromosomes, the haploid number (n). Each chromosome within a secondary spermatocyte, however, is made up of two chromatids (two copies of the DNA) still attached by a centromere. No replication of DNA occurs in the secondary spermatocytes. In meiosis II, the chromosomes line up in single file along the metaphase plate, and the two chromatids of each chromosome separate. The four haploid cells resulting from meiosis II are called spermatids. A single primary spermatocyte therefore produces four spermatids via two rounds of cell division (meiosis I and meiosis II). As spermatogenic cells proliferate, they fail to complete cytoplasmic separation (cytokinesis). The cells remain in contact via cytoplasmic bridges through their entire development. This pattern of development most likely accounts for the synchronized production of sperm in any given area of seminiferous tubule. It may also have survival value in that half of the sperm contain an X chromosome and half contain a Y chromosome. The larger X chromosome may carry genes needed for spermatogenesis that are lacking on the smaller Y chromosome. The final stage of spermatogenesis, spermiogenesis, is the development of haploid spermatids into sperm. No cell division occurs in spermiogenesis; each spermatid becomes a single sperm cell. During this process, spherical spermatids transform into elongated, slender sperm. An acrosome forms atop the nucleus which condenses and elongates, a flagellum develops, and mitochondria multiply. Sertoli cells dispose of the excess cytoplasm that sloughs off. Finally, sperm are released from their connections to Sertoli cells, an event known as Spermiation. Sperm then enter the lumen of the seminiferous tubule. Fluid secreted by Sertoli cells pushes sperm along their way, toward the ducts of the testes.

Storage of Sperm

The testes form up to 120 million sperms daily. A small quantity of these can be stored in the epididymis but most are stored in the vas deferens for at least a month where their fertility is maintained.

HORMONES AFFECTING SPERMATOGENESIS

Several hormones play essential role in spermatogenesis. Some of these are as follows:

1. **Testosterone**: It is secreted by the Leydig cells of the testis, and is essential for growth and division of the testicular germinal cells, which is the first stage in forming sperm.

2. **Luteinizing hormone**: It is secreted by the anterior pituitary gland. It stimulates the Leydig cells to secrete testosterone.

3. **Follicular-stimulating hormone**: It is also secreted by the anterior pituitary gland stimulates the Sertoli cells; without this stimulation, the conversion of the spermatids to sperm will not occur.

4. **Estrogens:** They are formed from testosterone by the Sertoli cells when they are stimulated by

follicular stimulating hormone. They are probably also essential for spermiogenesis.

5. **Growth hormone:** It is necessary for controlling background metabolic functions of the testes. It promotes early division of the spermatogonia themselves; in its absence (as in pituitary dwarfs) spermatogenesis is severely deficient or absent, thus causing infertility.

SPERMATOZOA (SPERM)

A sperm is about 60 μm long and contains several structures that are highly adapted for reaching and penetrating a secondary oocyte. The major parts of sperm are head and tail. The flattened, pointed head of the sperm is about 4-5 μm long. It contains a nucleus with 23 highly condensed chromosomes. The acrosome is covering the anterior two-third of the nucleus. It is a cap like vesicle filled with enzymes hyaluronidase and proteases that help sperm to penetrate secondary oocyte to bring about fertilization. The tail of sperm is subdivided into four parts: neck, middle piece, principal piece, and end piece. The neck is the constricted region just behind the head that contains centrioles. The centrioles form the microtubules that comprise the remainder of the tail. The middle piece contains mitochondria arranged in a spiral, which provide the energy (ATP) for motility and metabolism of sperm. The principal piece is the longest portion of the tail, and the end piece is the terminal, tapering portion. Once ejaculated, most sperm do not survive more than 48 hours within the female reproductive tract.

EPIDEMIOLOGY OF OLIGOSPERMIA

There is a geographical variation in the prevalence of male infertility with its prevalence amongst infertile couples being as high as 59 % in France, 26 % -32% in the United Kingdome and Kashmir Valley in India, and about 36 % in South Africa, Indonesia and Finland. Other studies indicated that there was also a regional variation in the mean sperm concentration in men from different regions of the USA and France. Geographic, ethnic, climatic and occupational factors have been suggested to be responsible for the regional differences in the sperm counts in men.

The prevalence of azoospermia and oligospermia in Mumbai, Bangalore and Jalandhar were similar to those reported in most other parts of the world. However, the prevalence of azoospermia in Kurnool (38.2 %) and Jodhpur (37.3 %) were Higher than those reported from any part of the world (Italy: 4.7 %; Siberia: 8.6 %; Indonesia: 12 %; Ethiopia: 26 %; Mexico: 19.9 %; Mongolia: 20 %; Nigeria: 6.4 % - 16 %; South Africa: 9 % and Zimbabwe: 24 %).

In the ancient Unani literature, following important causes of *Qillate Mani* are mentioned.

- *Zoafe badan* (generalised weakness) and *Kamie ghiza* (malnutrition).
- *Sue Mizaj barid* of *alate Mani* (gonads).'
- *Sue Mizaj haar* of *alate Mani.*
- *Sue Mizaj yabis* of *alate Mani.*'
- *Sue Mizaj ratab* of *alate Mani.*
- *Sue Mizaj barid yabis* of *alate Mani.*
- Use of drugs like *Afyoon* (opium) and *Bhang* (Cannabis).'
- *Kasrate istifragh*
- Excessive *ta'ab wa riyazat* (Fatigue and exercise)
- Excessive use of *mudirrat* (Diuretics)
- Excessive riding

Etiopathology

The causes of oligospermia mention in conventional system are as follows.

Idiopathic causes

In about 30% of all cases of Oligospermia the exact cause is unknown.This probably represents the end result of a multitude of ill-defined pathologies which disrupt normal seminiferous tubular functions. However, recent molecular analyses have revealed that a substantial proportion of these cases classified as idiopathic have discrete gene defects associated with impaired spermatogenesis. It may be caused by several factors such as chronic stress, endocrine disruption due to environmental pollution, reactive oxygen species and genetic abnormalities.

Hormonal causes

Hypothalamic disorder, Hypogonadism, Hyperprolactinemia, Hypothyroidism and Adrenal gland disorders etc.

Chromosomal Abnormalities

Klinefelter's Syndrome, reciprocal X or Y autosomal translocations, XYY and XX males, reciprocal and robertsonian autosomal translocations, supernumerary autosomes, inversion of autosomes and Y chromosome microdeletions.

Life style issues

Wearing tight under garments, working at high temperature places, sauna or hot tub use, extreme sports (marathon training), smoking and alcoholism.

Drugs

Drugs interfere with testicular function by several mechanisms including inhibition of testosterone synthesis (e.g. ketoconazole), blockade of androgen action (e.g. spironolactone), increased oestrogen (e.g. marijuana), or direct inhibition of spermatogenesis (e.g. chemotherapy). Cyclophosphamide causes azoospermia or extreme oligospermia within a few weeks after the initiation of therapy. Following drugs adversely affect spermatogenesis.

Methotrexate: It Damages germinal epithelium and sertoli cells.

5-alpha reductase inhibitors: They decrease serum dehydrotestoesterone levels.

Anabolic steroids: They interfere with the hypothalamo gonadal axis.

Ketoconazole: It reduces testosterone secretion.

Sufasalazine: It has anti-folate activity.

Oesterogen, Progesterogen: They reduce plasma gonadotrophin concentrations.

Akylating Agents: They cause testicular atrophy.

Gonadotoxins: Majority of chemicals adversely affect testicular function. They include alcohol, fungicides, insecticides, heavy metals, cottonseed oil and other environmental estrogens.

Cryptorchidism

Cryptorchidism occurs when there is incomplete descent of the testis from the abdominal cavity into the scrotum. About 3% of full-term and 30% of premature male infants have at least one cryptorchid testis at birth, but descent is usually complete by the first few weeks of life. Cryptorchidism is associated with increased risk of malignancy and infertility. Unilateral cryptorchidism, even when corrected before puberty, is associated with decreased sperm counts, possibly reflecting unrecognized damage to the fully descended testis.

Varicocoele

Varicocoele is the dilatation, elongation and tortuosity of the pampiniform plexus due to venous stasis. It is quite common and affects about 8-22% male in the general population but rises to 21-39% in men attending infertility clinic. Unrelieved venous stasis interferes with testicular temperature regulation which is usually maintained at 2-3°C less than core body temperature. Continuous exposure to high temperature causes sub-fertility by decreasing testicular volume, spermatogenesis, semen quality and an increase in immature sperm in the ejaculate.

Trauma to testes

Trauma including testicular torsion can also cause secondary atrophy of the testes.

Infections

Infections like tuberculosis, syphilis, mumps and gonorrhoea.

Orchitis

Viral orchitis may be caused by the mumps virus, echovirus, lymphocytic choriomeningitis virus, and group B arboviruses. Orchitis occurs in as many as one-fourth of adult men with mumps; the orchitis is unilateral in about two-third, and bilateral in the remainder. Orchitis usually develops a few days after the onset of parotitis but may precede it. The testis may return to normal size and function or undergo atrophy. Semen analysis returns to normal for three-fourths of men with unilateral involvement but normal for only one-third of men with bilateral orchitis.

Testicular tumours

It is important to remember that infertility can be a presenting symptom of testicular tumours, the commonest malignancy in young adult men. With increasing use of testicular ultrasound, it has become clear that there is a significantly higher risk of testicular tumours in infertile men (in the absence of cryptorchidism) compared to the general population. Carcinoma in situ, an obligatory precancerous state, is occasionally encountered incidentally in diagnostic testicular biopsies. Without treatment, 50 % of carcinomata in situ progress to malignant seminoma or non-seminomatous germ cell tumours.

Pelvic surgery

Pelvic surgeries like orchidopexy, inguinal hernia repair and vasectomy may cause damage to vascularisation and injury to vas deferens.

Radiation

The testes are sensitive to radiation damage. Doses >200 mGy (20 rad) are associated with increased

FSH and LH levels and damage to the spermatogonia. After ~800 mGy (80 rad), oligospermia or azoospermia develops, and higher doses may obliterate the germinal epithelium.

Sperm Antibodies

Sperm antibodies can cause isolated male infertility. In some instances, these antibodies are secondary phenomena resulting from duct obstruction or vasectomy. Granulomatous diseases (leprosy and tuberculosis) can affect the testes, and testicular atrophy occurs in 10 to 20% of men with lepromatous leprosy because of direct tissue invasion by the mycobacteria. The tubules are involved initially, followed by endarteritis and destruction of Leydig cells. Immunological infertility is a specific disorder caused by sperm membrane-bound IgA antibodies found in around 5 % of men presenting with infertility. Conditions predisposing to sperm autoimmunity include vasectomy, testicular injury/inflammation, genital tract infection/obstruction, and family history of autoimmune disease. Male patients with significant antisperm antibody titres usually have severely suppressed fertility potential due to sperm agglutination, poor sperm transit through cervical mucus, and blocked sperm–oocyte fusion.

The occupational Hazards

Many chemical agents exert the toxic effects on spermatogenesis. The known environmental hazards include microwaves, ultrasound and chemicals such as nematocide dibromochloropropane, cadmium, Benzene, Bromine vapour, Hydrocarbons and lead. In some populations sperm density is said to have declined by as much as 40% in the past years. Environmental estrogens or antiandrogens may be partly responsible. Working at high temperature places like welding, dyeing, blast furnace, cement and steel factories etc also affects adversely on the process of spermatogenesis.

Systemic disease

Systemic disease can cause primary testicular dysfunction in addition to suppressing gonadotrophin production. In cirrhosis, a combined testicular and pituitary abnormality leads to decreased testosterone production independent of the direct toxic effects of ethanol. Impaired hepatic extraction of adrenal androstenedione leads to extraglandular conversion to estrone and estradiol, which partially suppresses LH. Testicular atrophy and gynecomastia are present in approximately one half of men with cirrhosis.

In chronic renal failure androgen synthesis and sperm production decrease despite elevated gonadotrophins. The elevated LH level is due to reduced clearance, but it does not restore normal testosterone production. About one-fourth of men with renal failure have hyperprolactinemia. Improvement in testosterone production with haemodialysis is incomplete, but successful renal transplantation may return testicular function to normal. Testicular atrophy is present in one-third of men with sickle cell anaemia. The defect may be at either the testicular or the hypothalamic-pituitary level. Sperm density can decrease temporarily after acute febrile illness in the absence of a change in testosterone production.

Reactive Oxygen Species

Increased levels of reactive oxygen species can cause damage to the sperm membrane. Substances such as peroxidase and hydrogen peroxide can be released by abnormal sperm and by white blood cells, and when elevated levels of leukocytes are present in the semen (with a negative culture).

DIAGNOSIS

The single most important investigation for the diagnosis of Oligospermia is the semen analysis.

Semen analysis

Semen analysis is a core test in evaluation of male fertility status. For this test, the male is asked to abstain from ejaculation for 2 to 3 days, and a specimen is collected by masturbation into a sterile cup. If masturbation is not an option, then a couple can use specially designed Silastic condoms without lubricants. The sample undergoes liquefaction due to enzymatic action of the fluid from the prostate gland. This process takes 5 to 20 minutes and allows more accurate evaluation of the sperm contained in the seminal fluid. Ideally, two semen samples separated by at least a month should be analyzed. The reference values for the semen analysis are shown in table. The basic semen analysis measures semen volume, sperm concentration, sperm motility and sperm morphology.

Volume	>1.5 ml
Count	>20 million/ml
Motility	>50%
Normal Morphology	>30%

Semen volume

The normal ejaculated volume of semen is 2 to 6 ml. Volumes may be abnormally low in cases of retrograde ejaculation, and high volumes usually reflect relatively long periods of abstinence or inflammation of the accessory glands.

Sperm count

Sperm concentration or density is defined as the number of sperm /ml in the total ejaculate. Establishing a lower limit of normal for sperm concentration is difficult. Historically cut-off of 60 million sperm /ml for normal fertility has been advocated, but most WHO laboratories recognize the value of 20 million sperm /ml as a lower limit of normal.

Sperm motility

It is defined as the percentage of progressively motile sperm in the ejaculate. Lower limits of normal vary considerably and depend on the local laboratory's experience. The WHO and many laboratories use a cut-off of 50% motility as the lower limit of normal; whereas others require 40% motility as a criterion for defining male factor infertility. Computer-assisted semen analysis, in which computer-generated images of sperm specimens quantitate both sperm counts and sperm motility, may yield results very different from those of non-automated semen analyses. Some laboratories will distinguish between rapid (grade 3 to 4), slow (grade 2), and non-progressive (grade 0 to 1) movement. Total progressive motility is the percentage of sperm exhibiting forward movement (grades 2 to 4). Asthenospermia has been attributed to prolonged abstinence, presence of antisperm antibodies, genital tract infections, or varicocoele.

Sperm Morphology

Abnormal sperm morphology is termed as teratospermia. Many laboratories use the original classification in which normal morphology is characterized by over 50% of sperm exhibiting normal shape. More recently, Kruger and colleagues have developed strict criteria for defining normal morphology. Their studies defined a more detailed characterization of normal sperm morphology, with improved correlation with fertilization rates during IVF cycles. Their criteria require careful analysis of the shape and size of the sperm head, the relative size of the acrosome in proportion to the head, and characteristics of the tail, including length, coiling, or the presence of two tails. Fertilization rates are highest with normal morphology greater than 14%. Significantly decreased fertilization rates are seen when normal morphology falls to less than 4 %.

Other tests to know the cause of Oligospermia

Following investigations may be carried out to catch the exact cause of oligospermia.

Hormonal analysis

Hormonal testing in the male is analogous to endocrine testing in an anovulatory female. Essentially, abnormalities may be due to central defects in hypothalamic-pituitary function or to defects within the testes. Testing will include measurements of serum FSH, LH and testosterone (T) levels. Elevated FSH and low T levels provide an evidence of testicular failure. Alternatively, low FSH and low T levels are consistent with hypothalamic dysfunction, such as idiopathic hypogonadotropic hypogonadism or Kallman syndrome. A high LH and testosterone should raise the possibility of abnormalities in androgen receptors while low LH and testosterone suggest gonadotrophin deficiency.

Additional hormonal testing may be included as part of an evaluation of the infertile male. Elevated serum prolactin levels and thyroid dysfunction impact spermatogenesis and are the most likely endocrinopathies to be detected.

Testicular biopsy

Evaluation of a severely oligospermic or azoospermic male may include either open or percutaneous testicular biopsy to determine whether viable sperm are present in the seminiferous tubules. The biopsy specimen can be cryopreserved for future extraction of sperm during an IVF cycle. Thus, the biopsy may have diagnostic, prognostic and therapeutic value.

MANAGEMENT OF OLIGOSPERMIA

Oligospermia should be treated according to its etiologic factor.

Idiopathic Oligospermia

Although a wide variety of empirical medical treatments, including gonadotrophins, androgens, and anti-oestrogens, have been tried in attempts to improve fertility in men with Idiopathic Oligospermia, none have been shown to be effective when assessed in randomized, controlled therapeutic trials and are therefore not recommended. Instead, assisted conception techniques are increasingly applied to overcome idiopathic male infertility.

Drug induced Oligospermia

Removal or withdrawal of anti-spermatogenic agent or drug exposure may lead to improvement in fertility. This is most commonly seen in patients with inflammatory bowel diseases changing treatment from sulfasalazine to 5-aminosalicylic acid. Withdrawal from anabolic steroid abuse invariably leads to recovery of spermatogenesis although this may take many months because of the long half-lives of some preparations. Cryopreservation of semen should be offered to all male patients of reproductive ageing before commencing anticancer chemotherapy or testicular radiation.

Hypogonadotrophic hypogonadism

Patients with hypogonadotrophic hypogonadism should discontinue exogenous androgen replacement and start human chorionic gonadotrophin (hCG 2000 IU, subcutaneous, twice weekly) for 6 to 12 months. This should maintain normal testosterone levels. Patients with post-puberty acquired gonadotrophin deficiency (e.g. from pituitary tumour) where spermatogenesis has previously been established, usually respond to hCG treatment alone to reinitiate germ cell development. If there is no spermatozoa in the ejaculate at the end of 12 months, human menopausal gonadotrophin (hMG), which contain both FSH and LH, or recombinant FSH should be added at 75 to 150 IU, subcutaneous, thrice weekly. Combined treatment may be required for a further 12 months. Most patients with congenital forms of hypogonadotrophic hypogonadism will require FSH to stimulate Sertoli cell division and initiate spermatogenesis. In general, around 70 % should show active spermatogenesis and 50 % could be expected to achieve spontaneous pregnancies even if sperm densities remain in the oligospermic range. Patients with hypothalamic GnRH deficiency can be treated by pulsatile GnRH delivered 2-hourly by a battery-driven portable infusion minipump.

Infections

Active infection in the genital tract should be treated by appropriate antibiotics (erythromycin, doxycycline, norfloxacin) for 4 weeks for the patient and his partner.

Sperm antibody

Sperm antibody can be treated by immuno-suppression with high-dose prednisolone 0.75 mg/kg per day or prednisolone 20 mg twice daily on days 1 to 10 and 5 mg on days 11 and 12 of the partner's cycle for three to six cycles. Side-effects are irritability, sleeplessness, arthralgia, muscle weakness, peptic ulceration, glucose intolerance, and bilateral aseptic necrosis of femoral heads.

Varicocoele

Varicocoele can be treated either by open surgical ligation or trans-femoral embolization of the internal spermatic veins.

Life style issues

Avoid wearing tight underwear, working at high temperature places, sauna or hot tub use, extreme sports (marathon training, excessive strength sports). Give up any addiction like smoking, alcohol, cocaine and marijuana etc.

The occupational Hazards

Special precautions should be taken in people working occupations like welding, dyeing, blast furnace, cement and steel factories etc. Persons who usually come in contact with radiation like X-ray technicians should wear special shields.

USOOLE ILAJ WA ILAJ

Usoole Ilaj

- *Azalae sabab* (Removal of cause)
- *Muwallide Mani wa Mughallize mani advia* should be given.

Ilaj

The treatment of *Qillate Mani* will be as per the cause.

Zoafe badan and *kamie ghiza*

- *Latif kasiruttaghazya ghiza* should be given like *farbah gosht*, oily diet, *baize nim barisht* (half boiled eggs), dry fruits, *narjil maa shakar* (coconut with sugar) and *Halwae nishasta* etc.
- Abstinence from *Jima'a* (coitus).
- Keep the patient busy in *Aish wa ishrat* (luxuries) and *lah'wa laib* (entertainments).
- Excessive sleep will be advised.

- *Luboobe kabir* is thought to be better in this condition.

Sue Mizaj barid of alate Mani

- *Haar wa muqawwie bah* drugs will be given e.g. *Luboobe kabir, Muraabae Zanjaibil, Majoone Hilteet* etc.
- In diet *aabe nakhud* (gram water), *kunjashk* (flesh of sparrow), *kabutar bachcha* (flesh of dove), *murgh* (chicken) will be given. Add *Darchini, kababa and khulanjan* in the diet.

Sue Mizaj haar of alate Mani

- Treat with *mubarredat wa musakkine hararat advia* e.g. *Dawae hasak, Sheera tukhme khurfa*, milk and curd.
- Avoid *haar aghziya wa advia*.
- Apply *Roghane banafsha* over scrotum.
- Vegetarian diet will be advised.

Sue Mizaj yabis of alate Mani

- Treat with *murattebat* e.g. *Harerajat, muraghan shorba* and milk

- *Dawae Turanjabeen* will be given.

Sue Mizaj ratab of alate Mani

- *Mujaffif wa muskhkhin tadabir* should be adopted.
- *Zeera, Darchini, Itrifal Sagheer, Majoone Buzur* will be given.
- Add *mujaffifat* in the diet e.g. spices.

Sue Mizaj barid yabis of alate Mani

- *Haar ratab tadabir* will be adopted.
- *Hmmame moatadil* will be advised.
- *Darchini, Nukhud* will be added in the diet.
- Keep the patient busy in *farhat wa suroor* (happiness and entertainments).

Kasrate istifragh

- Those *tadabir* should be adopted that will help to replenish the lost *akhlat wa rutubat*.
- Perform *aabzan* in luke warm *joshanda* of *banafsha, baboona, nakhuna and nilofar*.

Others

Avoid excessive *riyazat*, *mudirrat* and riding.

COMMONLY USED MUFRAD ADVIA

Mufrad advia

- *Tukhme gazar,*
- *narjil taza,*
- *nakhud siyah,*
- *Baqla, Funduq*
- *Maghze chilghoza*
- *pyaz kham*
- *Bahman safaid*
- *Tukhme muli*
- *Bahman surkh*
- *Bozaidan*
- *Sheere gao*
- *Todari*
- *Salab misri*
- *Khurma*
- *Sighara*
- *Turanjabeen*
- *Tukhme shaljam*
- *Kharkahsak,*
- *Murgh*
- *Teetar bachcha*
- *Kabutar bachcha*

etc.

COMMONLY USED MURAKKAB ADVIA

Murakkab advia

- *Halwae Salab*

- *Halwae Nakhud alvi khan*

- *Dawae Turanjabeen*

- *Majoone Salab*

- *Johare khusiya*

- *Sufoofe Makhana*

- *Habbe Shaqaqul*

- *Majoone kishmish*

- *Dawae todriyaeen* etc.

SCIENTIFIC PROVEN DRUGS IN OLIGOSPERMIA

Talmakhana

Introduction

Talmakhana is seed of plant *Asteracantha longifolia* (L.) Nees which is the most commonly used aphrodisiac in Unani system of medicine since antiquity. The plant is widely distributed and cultivated in India and Srilanka. The seeds, root and leaves of plant are used for medicinal purposes. It contains essential oils, mucilage, alkaloids and important minerals like Ca, Mg, K, Fe, Cu, Zn etc; by virtue of which it has various aphrodisiac, hepatoprotective, diuretic and anticonvulsant activities. It is extensively used in Unani system of medicine for various therapeutic purposes like *Qillate Mani* (oligospermia), *Zoafe Bah* (sexual debility), *Surate inzale* (premature ejaculation), *Suddae Jigar* (hepatic obstructions), *Sozak* (gonorrhoea) *Wajaul Mafasil* (rheumatism) etc.

While in Ayurveda system of medicine it is known as Ikshura, Ikshugandha and Kokilasha, mentioned in 'Sushruta Samhita' and 'Charka Samhita' as Rasayan or rejuvenator and used for the management of neurodegenerative diseases and as immunomodulator, aphrodisiac and tonic agent. It is also scientifically proved that *Talmakhana* possesses diverse pharmacological actions which indicate its usefulness in the treatment of different types of diseases.

Botanical name

Asteracantha longifolia (L.) Nees / *Hygrophila spinosa* T Anders.

Family: Acanthaceae

Vernacular names

Urdu: Talmakhana

Hindi: Talmakhana

Assamese: Kulekhara

Marathi: Talimakhana

Kannada: Kolayalike

Bengali: Tuliakhara, Kamlakalika, Kuliakhara
               Bhikshu, Shrigali, Pushpa

Malayalam: Vayalculli

Oriya: Koillekha, Koilrekha

Punjabi: Talmakhana, Talimakhana

Sanskrit: Kakilaksha,Kolistha,   Ikshugandha, Atichhatra

Tamil: Nirmuli

Telugu: Neerugubbi

Kashmiri: Talimakhana, Talmakhana

Botanical Description

Asteracantha longifolia (L.) Nees is a herb growing in wet places. A stout herb; stems fasciculate, sub quadrangular, erect, 0.6-1.5 m tall, thickened at the nodes, hispid with long hairs; with axillary spines, leaves 9 × 1 cm, hairy, oblanceolate, in whorls. Flowers 2-3 cm long, purple-blue, bilabiate, in whorls. Fruits capsule, 8 mm long, 4-8 seeded, root is conical and hairy. Seeds are small, brown, 4.0 to 6.0 mm wide, much flattened and truncated at base, ovate-cordate in appearance, smooth when dry; if soaked in water and examined immediately under low power, adpressed trichomes star spreading and radiate all around the seeds except at the truncated part.

Af'aal: *Muwallide Mani, Mughallize Mani, Muqawwie bah, Mumsik, Musammine badan, Mudirre baul* and *Mufatteh suddade jigar wa tihal.*

Istemalat: *Zoafe bah, Surate inzal, Kasrate ehtelam, Sozak, Istisqa, Wajaul mafasil, Amraze azae baul, Yarqan, Suddae jigar wa tihal, Hasate kulliya, Hasate masana* and *Wajauz zahar*

Dose: 5-10 grams

Parts used: Seeds, root and leaves

Mizaj: Barid 2^0, Ratab 2^0

Muzarrat: *Naffakh, Der hazam*

Musleh: *Misri, Shahad khalis, Sheere gao, Qand safed*

Badal: *Musli, Satawar, Salab misri, Todari*

Compound formulations: *Halwae suparipak, Sufoofe muallif, Sufoofe beejband, Sufoofe jiryan* *khas, Majoone bahemanain* and *Majoone Talmakhana.*

Ethnobotanical description

Actions: Aphrodisiac, Anti-inflammatory, Diuretic, Demulcent and Tonic.

Uses: Dropsy, Rheumatism, Jaundice, Anasarca, Diarrhoea, Dysentery, Urinary calculi and Veneral diseases.

Chemical constituents

Seeds of *Talmakhana* contain mucilage, potassium salts, diastase, lipase, protease, sterols, alkaloids, fixed oils, fatty acids and minerals like Ca, Mg, K, Fe, Cu, Zn, Mn, Co and Cr.

Scientific Reports

Aphrodisiac activity: Chauhan NS et al in experimental study concluded that the ethanolic extract of *Talmakhana* seeds show androgenic activity as well as improved the sexual behaviour of rat in dose dependent manner, it also improves the histoarchitecture of testis and increase the concentration of sperm count in epididymis and also increase testosterone level.

Spermatogenic activity: Agrawal and Kulkarni conducted a clinical trial for which they recruited thirty male patients of infertility with oligospermia in the age group of 20-43 years. The patients were administered Speman (A polyherbal formulation containing *Asteracantha longifolia* as one of the ingredients) uncoated tablets at a dose of 2 tablets twice daily for the period of 6 months and were advised for follow-up every month. The complete semen analysis and serum testosterone levels were evaluated before and after the treatment. The results of the study showed that the speman is effective in oligospermia, as it increases the sperm count, improves its motility and morphology.

Antidiabetic activity: Muthulingam M et al conducted an experimental study to investigate the effect of aqueous extract of *Asteracantha longifolia* on alloxan induced diabetics in male albino Wistar rats. In their study the investigators concluded that *Asteracantha longifolia* leaf extracts proved to be effective in the treatment of diabetes mellitus.

Anthelminthic activity: Patra A et al evaluated the anthelminthic activity of petroleum ether, chloroform, alcohol and aqueous extracts of leaves of *Asteracantha longifolia* in different concentrations. Results of this study revealed that the alcoholic extract produced significant anthelminthic activity, whereas chloroform and aqueous extract showed moderate activity and petroleum ether extract was having the least anthelminthic activity.

Anti-bacterial activity: The antibacterial activity of petroleum ether, chloroform, alcohol, and aqueous extracts of leaves of *Asteracantha longifolia* were evaluated using disc diffusion method. Concentration of 100 mg/disc showed a significant increase in the diameters of the zone of inhibition (mm) for *Escherichia coli, Staphylococcus aureus, Bacillus subtilis* and *Pseudomonas aeruginosa* in petri dishes. This finding confirms its traditional use in bacterial infection.

Analgesic activity: In a study analgesic activity of *Asteracantha longifolia* leaves was studied using hot plate and tail flick by thermal method and acetic acid-induced writhing test in chemical method in mice. The petroleum ether, chloroform, alcohol, and aqueous extracts of leaves at a dose of 200 and 400 mg/kg of b.w. significantly increased the pain threshold of mice toward the thermal source in a dose dependent manner and also inhibited the abdominal constriction produced by acetic acid. This reveals its analgesic activity by central as well as peripheral mechanisms.

Anti-motility activity: Patra A et al in their study showed that the petroleum ether, chloroform, alcohol and aqueous leaf extracts of *Asteracantha longifolia* at a dose of 200 and 400 mg/kg expressed a dose dependent decrease in the distance travelled by charcoal meal through the gastrointestinal tract. This supports its traditional role in the treatment of diarrhoea and dysentery.

Hematopoietic activity: Hematopoietic activity of *Talmakhana* was evaluated by Pawar et al by using cyclophosphamide induced anaemia in rats. Chloroform extract of the leaves at both 250 and 500 mg/kg doses significantly improved RBC and haemoglobin counts for 7 days and cyclophosphamide induced bone marrow suppression after 21 days of treatment. It was also found that bone marrow cellularity was increased.

 Hepatoprotective activity: Hepatoprotective effect of aqueous extract of *Asteracantha longifolia* root was studied in carbon tetrachloride-induced liver damage albino rats by Usha et al. The aqueous extracts were administered for 15 days. The serum marker enzymes aspartate transaminase, alanine transaminase, and γ-glutamyl were measured. The increased enzyme levels after liver damage with carbon tetrachloride were nearing normal value when treated with aqueous extract of the root samples. Histopathology observation was also supportive to the hepatoprotective activity of the root samples.

Diuretic activity: In an experimental study the diuretic activity of different fraction of *Talmakhana* was performed in male Wistar albino rats in comparison to frusemide. Alcoholic extract and n-butanol fraction showed significantly good diuretic action and electrolytic excretion of Na^+ and K^+ without significant renal excretion of Cl^- as compared to frusemide. The diuretic actions of other fractions like petroleum ether, chloroform and ethylacetate were not significant.

Salab misri

Introduction

Salab misri (*Orchis latifolia*) is an important medicinal plant found throughout Kashmir to Nepal at an altitude of 2500-5000 m in damp places. It is cultivated in Europe, India and north Asia. Fresh root tubers give a seminal smell. It has been used as an aphrodisiac drug since long in Unani as well as Ayurveda. It has important pharmacological actions like aphrodisiac, nervine tonic, nutritive, astringent and diuretic; and is widely used in treatment of syphilis, diarrhoea, strangury and tuberculosis etc. Chemical analysis of *Salab misri* reveals that it contains mucilage, protein and volatile oils etc .

Botanical name: *Orchis latifolia* Linn.

Family: Orchidaceae

Vernacular names

Arabic: Khussiyatus Salab, Salab misri

Persian: Khana rubah

Sanskrit:	Salampamisri, Munjatakah
English:	Salep, Marh orchid
Urdu:	Salab misri
Hindi:	Salam panja, Salab misri
Marathi:	Sala misri
Telugu:	Goru-chettu
Kanada:	Salamisri
Bengali:	Salamisri
Tamil:	Sala misri

Botanical Description

Salab misri consists of dried root tubers of plant *Orchis latifolia* which is tuberous terrestrial orchid with stems 30-90 cm in height, leaves many, erect, oblong or lanceolate; flowers dull purple in cylinderic spikes, sepals and petals acute or obtuse, lip oblong or rhomboid. Root tubers are palmate or simple, creamish white in colour, 5 cm in length and up to 3 cm wide, often pointed at lower end and rounded at the upper, where occurs a depressed scar, left by the remains of the stem. Tuber is generally shrunken, contorted covered with a rough granular skin, translucent very hard and horny; fracture is short and granular; fractured surfaces is shiny, yellowish-white. Palmate tubers are yellowish-white or deep yellow in colour, having 3-5 digits, usually broken; sweet in taste with a mucilaginous feel.

Af'aal: *Mughallize Mani, Muwallide Mani, Mumsik Muqawwie Bah, Muqawwie Aasab, Nafae falij wa laqwa, Musammine Badan* and *Muhallile Warame Balghami.*

Istemalat: *Zoafe Bah, Kuzaz, Tashannuj, Falij, Tamaddud, Laqwa, Qulae dahan, Uqar , Qillate Mani, Surate Inzal, Jiryan* and *Qillate haiwane manviya.*

Dose: 4 gms, 3-5 gms

Parts used: Root

Mizaj: Haar 1^0 Ratab 1^0

Muzarrat: For Haar Mizaj people, Jigar, Riya (Lungs) and Fame Meda.

Musleh: *Sikanjabeen, Samaghe Arabi*

Badal: *Bozidan*

Compound formulations: *Majoone Falasfa, Sufoofe Salab, Habbe Mumsik, Habbe Ambar momyai, Halwae Salab, Halwae Ghekwar, Sufoofe Muallif, Lubube Kabir, Majoone Suparipak* and *Majoone Mughalliz sada.*

Ethnobotanical description

Actions: Aphrodisiac, Nervine tonic, Nutritive, Astringent, Diuretic, Refrigerant, Antidiarrhhoeal, Anthelmintic, Analgesic, Tonic and Expectorant.

Uses: Sexual Debility, Diarrhoea, Chronic dysentery, Tuberculosis, Strangury, Syphilis, Otalgia, Cephalgia and Helminthiasis.

Chemical constituents: *Salab misri* contains mucilage (Up to 50%), glucans, glucomannas, starch (25%), protein (5-15%), volatile oil, bitter substances and glucosides.

Scientific Reports

Sexual stimulant activity: The aqueous extract of *Orchis latifolia* rich in fructooligosaccharides (FOS's) as well as phytosterols were evaluated for their efficacy against streptozotocin and alloxan (Hyperglycaemic agents) induced sexual dysfunction. The behavioural analysis of rats was undertaken to observe the effect on mount, ejaculation and intromission latencies as well as frequencies, hesitation time and copulatory rate. It was observed that hyperglycaemia has an adverse effect on overall sexual behaviour. The harmful effect was significantly reduced in animals treated with polysaccharide rich fraction of *O. latifolia*. The study suggests that the diabetes induced sexual disability may be ameliorated by proper usage of herbal drugs.

Aphrodisiac activity: A laboratory study was conducted on adult Swiss male mice to assess the aphrodisiac and spermatogenic activity of *Orchis latifolia*. After completion of trial it was found that there was remarkable increase in the organ weights as well as sperm counts in experimental group than the control (placebo) group. There was also significant increase in the protein, haemoglobin and testosterone content; whereas there was significant decrease in total cholesterol content in the experimental groups that of the control (placebo) group.

Spermatogenic activity: In a clinical trial thirty male patients of oligospermia with infertility were recruited. The patients were administered Speman (A polyherbal formulation containing *Salab misri* as one of the ingredients) uncoated tablets at a dose of 2 tablets twice daily for the period of 6 months and were advised for follow-up every month. The complete semen analysis and serum testosterone levels were evaluated before and after the treatment. The results of the study showed that speman is effective in oligospermia, as it increases the sperm count, improves its motility and morphology.

Mahesh Shah reported a case of primary infertility to which he treated with tentex forte (A polyherbal formulation containing *Salab misri* as one of the ingredients) remarkable results were obtained with tentex forte therapy shows impressive progress in sperm count and motility.

Antihypertensive Action: A study was conducted by Nauman Aziz et al to investigate the possible modes of action for the medicinal use of *Salab misri* in hypertension. It was found that in spontaneously hypertensive rats, it significantly reduced systolic blood pressure and improved endothelial dysfunction by increasing acetylcholine-induced relaxation. And in normotensive anaesthetized rats, the crude extract of *Salab misri* caused a dose-dependent attenuation of mean arterial pressure.

Singhara

Introduction

Singhara commonly known as water chestnut is a fruit obtained from an aquatic herb occurring throughout the greater parts of India in lakes, tanks and ponds. It is commercially cultivated across different parts of India for its consumable seasonal fruits. Traditionally the plant has been used as nutritive, astringent, aphrodisiac, cooling, appetizer, tonic and antidiarrhhoeal agent etc. In Unani system of medicine it has been used in the treatment of sexual weakness, tuberculosis, bilious affections, bronchitis and renal calculi, etc. Chemical analysis of *Singhara* reported its different constituents such as carbohydrates, proteins and important vitamins like thiamine, riboflavin, pantothenic acid, pyridoxine etc.

Recent experimental and clinical studies exhibited its different pharmacological actions analgesic, antibacterial, immunomodulator, antidiabetic and antiulcer activities etc.

Botanical name: *Trapa bispinosa* Roxb.

Family: Trapaceae

Vernacular names

English: Water chest nut

Bengali: Paniphal

Persian: Singhara

Gujarati: Singora

Hindi: Simghara, Simghada

Kanada: Singara

Malayalam: Karimpolam, Vankottakkaya

Marathi: Shingade

Sanskrit: Smgtakah, Jalphala

Tamil: Chimkhara

Telugu: Kubjakamu

Urdu: Singhara

Botanical Description

It is an annual aquatic floating herb found in lakes and ponds. Stems are flexuous and ascending while root is green submerged photosynthetic. Floating leaves are rhomboid in shape, petiolate with a truncated base, entire acute glaucous above, villous tomentose beneath. Flowers are white. Fruit is obovoid triangular in shape with two horns one seeded, green in fresh condition but after drying it becomes blackish. The pulp of the fruit is whitish, sweet in taste.

Af'aal: *Muwallide mani, Mughallize mani, Muqawwie bah, Muqawwie aam, Nafe tape Safravi wa damvi, Nafae tape dique, Mushtahi, Mujallie dandan, Muqawwie lissa, Habisuddam, Nafae zaheer, Musakkine hararat, Qabiz, Habis, Muallide riyah* and *Mughazzi.*

Istemalat: *Zoafe bah, Jiryane mani, Zoafe aam, Tape dique, Tape safravi, Khashunate halaque, Nasure miqad, Zaheer, Is'haal, Joshe khoon, Laghari, Nazafuddam* and *Suaale haar.*

Dose: 3 to 10 grams

Parts used: Fresh and dried fruits

Mizaj:

Fresh: Barid ratab 1^0

Dried: Barid yabis 1^0

Muzarrat: For *barid Mizaj* persons, *Der hazam, Musaddid, Saqeel*

Musleh: *Shakar, Mirch siyah*

Compound formulations: *Majoon Arade khurma, Sufoofe muallif, Sufoofe kalan* and *Halwae suparipak.*

Ethnobotanical description

Actions: Aphrodisiac, astringent, appetizer, antipyretic, cooling, constipating, diuretic, tonic and haemostatic.

Uses: Dyspepsia, diarrhoea, dysentery, strangury, intermittent fevers, leprosy, pharyngitis, lumbago, bronchitis, sore throat generalised debility, haemorrhages, erysipelas threatened abortion, dysuria, polyuria and oedema.

Chemical constituents

Organic materials: It contains carbohydrates and vitamins like Vitamin B-complex (thiamine, riboflavin, pantothenic acid, pyridoxine, nicotinic acid), Vitamin-C, Vitamin -A, D-amylase and considerable amount of phosphorylase.

Inorganic materials: Acids, minerals matters, calcium, phosphate, iron, copper, manganese, magnesium, sodium and potassium.

Scientific Reports

Analgesic activity: An experimental study conducted by K Anuj et al, analgesic activity of the methanolic extract of the *T. bispinosa* root at a dose of 200mg/kg and 400mg/kg was evaluated against the standard drug pentazocine at a dose of 30mg/kg. Adult Swiss albino mice of either sex of six numbers in each group was undertaken for study and evaluated by tail flick and tail immersion method. The both doses of *T. bispinosa* roots methanolic extract were found to produce significant analgesic activity. The results showed significant analgesic activity against stimuli.

Antibacterial activity: Mohammad A Razvy et al were studied antibacterial activities of the fruit extract of two varieties (Green and red Varieties) of water chestnut by the disc diffusion method from methanol extract. The extract of red variety of water chestnut showed high antibacterial potential (31mm) against *Bacillus subtilis* with the concentration of 600 micron. On the other hand, green variety showed highest antibacterial activities (12mm) against both *Staphylococcus aureus* and *Shigella sonnei* with the concentration of 600microgram kanamycin used as standard. In this disc diffusion assay, the methanol extract of red variety was found to have a significant antibacterial activity than the extract of green variety of water chestnut. These findings pointed out the effect of these extracts to inhibit microbial growth.

Antidiabetic activity: In an animal trial conducted by K Das Parshanto et al antidiabetic activity of methanol extract of *Singhara* fruit peels were studied in Wistar rats. Its effect on oral glucose tolerance and on normoglycaemic rats was studied. It was found that at the dose of 100 and 200 mg/kg orally, *Singhara* significantly and dose dependently improved oral glucose tolerance, exhibited hypoglycaemic effect in normal rats and antidiabetic activity in STZ-induced diabetic rats by reducing and normalizing the elevated fasting blood glucose levels as compared to those of STZ control group.

Anti-ulcer activity: Kar DM et al studied the antiulcer activity of the fruits of *Trapa bispinosa* on Wistar rats. The antiulcer activity of 50% ethanolic extract at two dose levels was evaluated by using pyloric ligation and aspirin plus pyloric ligation models. The tests extract revealed significant antiulcer activity, which might be due to increase in total carbohydrate content and alter state of mucosal barrier of the stomach. The results indicate that the ethanolic extract of fruits of *Trapa bispinosa* is endowed with potential antiulcer activity.

Neuroprotective activity: In a study the effect of hydroalcoholic extract of *Trapa bispinosa* was studied on fluorescence product and biochemical parameter like lipid peroxidation, catalase activity and glutathione peroxidase activity in brain of female albino mice. Ageing was accelerated by the treatment of 0.5ml 5% D-galactose for 15 days. This resulted in increased fluorescence product, increase lipid peroxidation and decrease antioxidant enzyme like glutathione peroxidase and catalase in cerebral cortex. After co-treatment with hydroalcoholic extract of *Trapa bispinosa* there was decrease in fluorescence product in cerebral cortex. Moreover, *T.bispinosa* inhibited increase lipid peroxidation and restores glutathione peroxidase and catalase activity in cerebral cortex as compare to ageing accelerated control group. To conclude *T.bispinosa* found to be effective anti-oxidative agent which could to some extent reverse D-galactose induced ageing changes resulted due to oxidative damage.

Immunomodulatory Potential: An experimental study was conducted to assess the immunomodulatory effect in rats against sheep red blood cells (SRBC) as antigen by studying cell-mediated delayed type hypersensitivity reaction, humoral immunity response and percent change in neutrophil count. Oral administration of aqueous extract of fruits of *T.bispinosa* dose dependently increased immunostimulatory response. The result of this study suggests that aqueous extract of fruits of *T. bispinosa* could stimulate the cellular and humoural response in animals and it deserves further researches to develop an immuno-stimulating agent among herbal origin.

Neuropharmacological activity: In a study conducted by NS Vyawahare the different doses (100,250,500mg/kg, p.o) of hydroalcoholic extract of *Trapa bispinosa* (TB) were administered in laboratory animals. The effects of extract on various parameters like motor coordination, spontaneous locomotor activity, object recognition, transfer latency, anxiolytic activity, sodium nitrite induced respiratory arrest and hypoxic stress etc were studied. The *T.bispinosa* (250 and 500mg/kg) found to decrease time required to occupy the central platform (transfer latency) in the elevated plus maze and to increase discrimination index in the object recognition test, indicating nootropic activity. TB (250,500 mg/kg) showed significant increase in reaction time in hot plate analgesic activity. Moreover it also showed significant reduction in spontaneous locomotory activity and latency memory which may be due to enhanced cholinergic function. It also showed significant analgesic activity.

Gonde kekar

Introduction

Gonde kekar (*Samaghe arabi*) is a dried gum obtained from the stem and branches of the plant Acacia *arabica*. It is commonly found all over the India in dry and sandy areas; plentiful in western peninsula, the Deccan and Coromandal Coast. Chemically *Gonde Kekar* contains galactose, L-arabinose, L-rhamnose and four aldobiouronic acids. It is used for preparation of various Unani formulations as a binder. It is widely used in the treatment of several diseases such as spermatorrhoea, leucorrhoea, sore throat and diarrhoea etc.

Botanical name: *Acacia arabica* Willd.

Family: Mimosaceae

Vernacular names

English: Gum Acacia, Indian Gum Arabica

Arabic:	Samaghe Arabi, Aqaqia
Persian:	Mugilan
Urdu:	Babul
Hindi:	Babul, Kekar
Sanskrit:	Babbula, Vabboola
Kannada:	Gobbli
Marathi:	Babul
Tamil:	Karuvael
Telugu:	Nallatumma
Malayalam:	Kruvelum
Bengali:	Babla

Description of drug

It is dried gummy exudation obtained from the stem and branches of Babul tree. It occurs in the form of rounded to ovoid tears. Each tear is about a centimeter in size. The colour varies from pale to yellow or brown or almost black, according to the age of the tree and the condition of collection. Gum is of two types white and red. White is considered as good quality gum. This gum is brittle in nature, irregular tears of varying size. It is mucilaginous odourless. It is insoluble in alcohol and oil but soluble in water. The gum is first broken into small pieces, cleaned and stored according to size and colour. It is considered as strong and best quality in all type of gums.

Af'aal: *Qabiz, Habis, Mujaffif, Habis ishaal, Muqawwi meda wa amaa, Mulattif, Mulayyan sadar, Mujammid, Tiryaq* and *Mugherry.*

Istemalat: *Jiryan, Sailanur rahem, Khushunate Halaque, Pechish, Sil, Is'hal* and *Suaal.*

Dose: 1-3 gms, 3-6 gms.

Parts used: Gum, bark, leaves, flowers, pods and wood

Mizaj: *Motadil* in *Harat* and *Barudat* and *Yabis* in $2°$

Muzarrat: Harmful for rectum, constipative

Musleh: *Kateera Sandal, Gulab*

Badal: *Kateera, Gond Dhak , Habbul Aas*

Compound formulations: *Habbe Jadwar, Habbe Ral, Habbe Momyai sada, Sufoofe Muallif, Qurse habis, Qurse Sozak, Majoone Arade Khurma* and *Majoone Zanjabeel.*

Ethnobotanical description

Actions: Aphrodisiac, Demulcent, Tonic, Haemostat, Antitussive, Expectorant, Decongestant, Antihistaminic, Anti-inflammatory, Astringent and Styptic.

Therapeutic uses: Cough, Cholera, Diarrhoea, Diabetes mellitus, Dysentery, Dyspepsia, Haemorrhage, Leucorrhoea, Strangury, Sexual debility, Tuberculosis and Pharyngitis.

Chemical constituents: *Gonde kekar* contains galactose, L-arabinose, L-rhamnose and four aldobiouronic acids. It also contains arabinobios, 3-o-β-arabinopyranosyl-L-arabinose.

Scientific Reports

Antiplaque Activity: Two blind crossover trials were carried out to evaluate the antiplaque potential of Acacia gum compared with sugar free gum. In first trial, the mean gingival and plaque scores were lower after 7 days of using Acacia compared with sugar-free gum but the differences were insignificant. In second trial, daily photographic assessment of erythrocine-stained plaque showed lower scores after Acacia gum compared with sugar-free gum. The total difference in scores for each day from each individual between the two treatment groups was highly significant. This implies the presence of substances in Acacia gum which compared with ordinary gum primarily inhibit the early deposition of plaque.

Antioxidant: Trommer and Neubert studied eight different polysaccharide compounds (including Gum Acacia) for their antioxidant and lipid peroxidation lowering effects in vitro. It was found that Gum Acacia protected against lipid peroxidation in skin in a dose-dependent manner.

Antibacterial activity: DT Clark et al assessed the antibacterial activity of acacia gum using fresh isolates and reference strains of *Actinobacillus actinomycetemcomitans, Capnocytophga spp., Porphyomonas gingivalis, Prevotella intermedia* and *Treponema denyicola*. In this study it is concluded that the acacia gum has good action against periodontal pathogens and their enzymes.

Hypoglycemic effect: Wadood A et al conducted an experimental study on normal rabbits and rabbits with alloxan induced diabetes and administered powdered seeds of *Acacia arabica* orally. It was found that the powder (at doses of 2, 3 and 4 mg/kg) significantly reduced the blood glucose concentration of normal, but not in diabetic rabbits. The authors concluded, albeit without experimental evidence that *A. arabica* initiated the release of insulin from pancreatic β cells of normal rabbits.

Mazu sabz

Introduction

Mazu sabz (Oak galls, Turkish galls) is the dried galls which are excrescences (projections) formed as a result of stimulus produced by the larva of the gall wasp *Adleria gallaetinctoriae*, and found on twigs of dyer's oak (*Quercus infectoria* Olive.), a medium sized tree occurring in Greece, Bosnia, Turkey, Syria and Persia. In Unani system of medicine it has been used since ancient times for various therapeutic purposes preferably for gingivitis, leucorrhoea, wounds, rectal and uterine prolapse and bleeding disorders etc. *Mazu* contains 50-70% of the tannin known as gallotannic acid. Several pharmacological studies have been carried out on *Mazu* which explored its different actions such as antibacterial, antidiabetic and wound healing activities etc.

Botanical name: *Quercus infectoria* Olivier

Family: Fagaceae

Vernacular names

Arabic: Ufas

Unani: Iqaqualees

Urdu: Mazu

Persian: Mazu

English: Oak galls, Turkey galls

Sanskrit: Maju phal

Hindi: Mazu, Mazuphal

Marathi: Maiphala

Guajarati: Mayaphal

Kannada: Machikai

Talugu: Machikaya

Tamil: Mashikai

Malayalam: Majakani

Bengali: Majuphal

Botanical Description

Mazu sabz is usually found in globular shape and ranges from 10 to 25 mm in diameter. It has a short, basal stalk and numerous rounded projections on the surface. It is hard and heavy, usually sinking in water. The 'blue' variety is actually of a grey or brownish-grey colour. This and to a lesser extent the olive-green 'green' galls, are preferred to the 'white' variety, in which the tannin is said to have been partly decomposed. White galls also differ from the other grades in having a circular tunnel through which the insect has emerged. *Mazu sabz* without the opening has insect remains in the small central cavity. It has a very astringent taste and non specific odour.

Sections through a gall show a very large outer zone of thin walled parenchyma, a ring of sclernchymatous cells, and a small, inner zone of rather thick-walled parenchyma surrounding the central cavity. The parenchymatous tissues contain abundant starch, masses of tannin, rosettes and prisms of calcium oxalate, and the rounded so called 'Lignin bodies', which give a red colour with phloroglucinol and hydrochloric acid.

Af'aal: *Habise Haiz, Qabiz, Mane Ruaaf, habisuddam, Dafae Taffun, Mujaffif* and *Muqawwie Danda wa lissa.*

Istemalat: *Irqe mufrit, Qarhae amaa, Is'hale kuhna, Qulae dahan, Warame lissa, Istirkhae luhat, Namla, aakela, Dad, Daus Salab, Jhaein, Salaque, Damaa(Dhalka),Ruaaf, Kasrate Haez, Baolud Dam, Khuruje Miqad, Warame Miqad, Quruhe Miqad, Sailanur Raham, Khuruje Raham , Bawasire Damavi* and *Jarabe aain.*

Dose: 3-5 gms, 4 gms

Parts used: Excrescence, Fruit

Mizaj: *Barid* 1^0 *Yabis* 2^0, *Barid* 2^0 *Yabis* 3^0 ˒

Muzarrat: For *Sadar wa Halaque* (chest and throat)

Musleh: *Katira, Samaghe Arabi, Zardie Baizae neem barisht*

Badal: *Maei khurd wa kalan, Poste Anaar*

Compound formulations: *Majoon Muqawwi Rahem , Sufoofe Habis, Sufoofe muallif, Sunoone zarad, Sunoone muqawwie dandan, Qurse bandishe khoon* and *Majoone Hamal ambary alvi khani.*

Ethnobotanical description

Actions: Astringent, Analgesic, Antidote, Hypnotic, Hypoglycaemic, Sedative and Tonic.

Uses: Bleeding, Bronchitis, Carcinoma, Cough, Diabetes, Diarrhoea Dysentery, Eczema, Fever, Gingivitis, Gonorrhoea, Haemoptysis, Impetigo, Hyperhydrosis, Leucorrhoea, Malaria, Menorrhagia, Pharyngitis, Polyp, Prolapse, Stomatosis, Tonsillitis, Wart and Wound.

Chemical constituents: *Mazu* contains 50-70% of the tannin known as gallotannic acid. This is a complex mixture of phenolic acid glycosides varying greatly in composition. It is prepared by fermenting the galls and extracting with water-saturated ether. *Mazu* also contains gallic acid (about 2-4%), ellagic acid, sitosterol, methyl betulate, methyloleanolate, starch and calcium oxalate. Nyctanthic, roburic and syringic acids have more recently been identified as the CNS- active component of the methanolic extract of galls. Tannic acid is hydrolysable tannin yielding gallic acid and glucose and having the minimum complexity of pentadigalloyl glucose. Solutions of tannic acid tend to decompose on keeping with formation of gallicacid, a substance which is also found in many commercial samples of tannic acid. It may be detected by the pink colour produced on the addition of a 5% solution of potassium cyanide .

Scientific Reports

Antibacterial activity: In a study mechanism of *Quercus infectoria* extract and its components were investigated for anti-methicillin-resistant Staphylococcus aureus. The appearance of pseudomulticellular bacteria in the treated cells and the synergistic effect of the plant extract with beta-lactamase-susceptible penicillins suggest that the extract may interfere with staphylococcal enzymes including autolysins and beta-lactamase. This study results provide scientific data on the use of the oak galls, which contain mainly tannin contents up to 70% for the treatment of staphylococcal infections.

Wound healing effect: An experimental trial conducted by SP Umachigi et al, the ethanol extract of the shade-dried leaves of *Quercus infectoria* was studied for its effect on wound healing in rats, using incision, excision and dead-space wound models, at two different dose levels of 400 and 800 mg/kg. The plant showed a definite, positive effect on wound healing, with a significant increase in the levels of the antioxidant enzymes, superoxide dismutase and catalase, in the granuloma tissue. The efficacy of this plant in wound healing may be due to its action on antioxidant enzymes, thereby justifying the traditional claim.

Antidiabetic activity: R Saini et al tested the methanolic extract of roots of *Quercus infectoria* Olivier at a dose of 250 mg/kg and 500 mg/kg body weight respectively for anti-diabetic activity in Alloxan-induced hyperglycaemic rats. The blood glucose levels were measured at 0, 2h, 4h and 6h after the treatment. The methanolic extract reduced the blood glucose Alloxan- induced diabetic rats from 285.52 to 206.57mg/dl, 6h after oral administration of extract. The antidiabetic activity of methanolic extract of *Quercus infectoria* Olivier was compared with glibenclamide, an oral hypoglycaemic agent (3mg/kg).

Anti-inflammatory action: Effect of alcoholic extract of *Q. infectoria* galls was evaluated on various experimental models of inflammation. Oral administration of gall extract significantly inhibited carrageenan, histamine, serotonin and prostaglandin E_2 (PGE_2) induced paw oedemas, while topical application of gall extract inhibited phorbol-12-myristate-13-acetate (PMA) induced ear inflammation. The extract also inhibited various functions of macrophages and neutrophils relevant to the inflammatory response.

Larvicidal effect: Aivaazi AA et al made an effort to assay *Anopheles stephensi* larvae with gall extracts of *Quercus infectoria* under laboratory conditions at Mysore. Ethyl-acetate extract was found to be the most effective of all the five extracts tested for larvicidal activity against the fourth instar larvae, with LC (50) of 116.92 ppm followed by gallotannin, n-butanol, acetone, and methanol with LC (50) values of 124.62, 174.76, 299.26, and 364.61 ppm, respectively. The efficacy in killing mosquito larvae may make this plant promising for the development of new botanical larvicide.

Analgesic activity: A fraction of methanol extract of galls showed analgesic activity in rats and significantly reduces blood pressure in rabbits. Another fraction showed CNS depressant activity and moderate anti-tremorine activity by causing a delay in onset and decrease in severity of tremorine-induced tremors. It also showed anaesthetic action due to complete blockade of isolated frog sciatic nerve conduction.

Antioxidant activity: Kaur G et al studied the antioxidant activity of ethanolic extract of *Quercus infectoria* galls was by employing several established in vitro model systems. Their protective efficacy on oxidative modulation of murine macrophages was also explored. Gall extract was found to contain a large amount of polyphenols and possess a potent reducing power. The results indicate that *Q. infectoria* galls possess potent antioxidant activity, when tested both in chemical as well as biological models.

Mastagi rumi

Introduction

The drug *Mastagi* is a resin obtained from *Pistacia lentiscus* Linn., a shrub or small tree indigenous to Mediterranean areas specially Spain, Portugal, Morocco, Italy, Greece, Turkey and southern France. *Pistacia lentiscus* L. is an aromatic member of the Anarcadiaceae family. The Unani physicians has been using *Mastagi* since ancient times for the treatment of many ailments like gastrointestinal disturbances, Hepatobiliary disorders, gynaecological diseases, fractures, wounds and ENT problems. Chemically *Mastagi* contains resins, volatile oils, terpenoids and fatty acids. Several pharmacological studies have also reported that essential oil from *P. lentiscus* possesses appreciable biological properties such as antifungal, antibacterial and antimicrobial. Apart from it many experimental studies proved its anti-inflammatory, antioxidant, antiatherogenic and wound healing properties.

Botanical name: *Pistacia lentiscus* Linn.

Family: Anarcadiaceae

Vernacular names

Arabic: Alake rumi, Mastaki

Persian: Kundur rumi

Urdu: Rumec Mastagi

Hindi: Rumi Mastagi, Mastagi

English: Mastic, Mastiche

Bengali: Rumi Mastungi

Gujrati: Rumi Mastagee

Marathi: Rumaa Mastakee

Botanical Description

Mastagi is resinous exudation obtained by incision from the stems of the plant *Pistacia lentiscus* Linn. The best *Mastagi* occurs in roundish tears about the size of 2 to 8 mm in diameter, or in more or less flattened or irregular oblong or pear shaped pieces; which are externally covered with a light whitish powder from their mutual attrition. The tears have pale yellow colour which darkens by age, they are somewhat opaque on their surface but quite transparent in their interior; they are brittle and break with a conchoidal vitrous fracture, taste is slightly agreeable and odour is aromatic.

Af'aal: *Muqawwie Meda wa jigar, Kasire Riyah, Mulaiyin, Munaffise Balgham, Mulattif, Muhallile Aauram, Jazibe Rutubat, Jaali, Qabiz, Habisuddam, Muqawwie Aazae Raeesa, Muqawwie Gurda, Dafae Qae, Mujallie Dandan, Dafae Istirkha, Nafae Istisqa, Mudammile Quruh, Mushtahi, Muqawwie lissa, Muqawwie Hafeza* and *Mudirre Baul.*

Istemalat: *Jiryan, Busure jild, Quruhe Saaeiyah, Takassure Ezam, Suaal, Nafasuddam, Nafakhe shikam, Aurame Meda, Zusantariya, Sahaje amaa, Aurame Jigar, Malankhuliya, Kazaz, ra'asha, Khuruje Rahem, Khuruje Miq'ad, Muzmin Sailanurrahem, Quruhe khabisa, Taqash'shure*

Shafataen, Tahabbuj, Pechish, Sudaa, Istaquae Ziqui,Zoafe Meda and *Zoafe Jigar*.

Dose: Upto 4 gms

Parts used: Resinous exudates,

Mizaj: Har 2^0, Yabis 2^0

Muzarrat: For *Masana* (Urinary bladder)

Musleh: *Smaghe arabi, Guke surkh, Maghze Akhrot*

Badal: *Kundur* in equal quantity, *Alake Bat'm* in 1 ½ quantity

Compound formulations: *Jawarishe* Jalinoos, *Jawahar mohra, Habbe Ambar Momyai, Habbe Mumsik Ambari, Sufoofe Muhafize janeen, Sufoofe Muallif, Luboobe Kabir, Majoone Azaraqi, Majoone Barhami* and *Majoone Mughalliz sada*.

Ethnobotanical description

Actions: Aphrodisiac, Analgesic, Antibacterial, Antiseptic, Antitumour, Antiulcer, Antitussive,

Appetizer, Astringent, Carminative, Hemostatic, Laxative, Stomachic, Hypotensive, Fungicide, Candidicide, Antisarcomic, Stimulant, Diuretic, Expectorant and Antidiarrhoeal.

Uses: Bronchitis, Cough, Diarrhoea, Boils, Ulcers, lymph adenopathy, Bacterial infections, Anorexia, Bleeding, Candidiasis, Carbuncle, Dental carries, Cirrhosis, Constipation, Dysentery, Gonorrhoea, Leucorrhoea and Rheumatism.

Chemical constituents: *Mastagi* contains resin, volatile oil, bicyclic terpenoids, fatty acids; α-pinene, β- pinene, limonene, terpenin-4-ol and α-terpenoil are major components. The resin is divided into two types one which is soluble in alcohol and ether is termed as alpha resin of mastich, it is 90% of total resin, it is acidic in nature hence called as masticic acid; while other one which is not soluble in alcohol is called as beta resin of mastic or masticin, it is10%.

Antiatherogenic action: Dedoussis GV et al conducted a laboratory study in which they proved that glutathione restoration and down regulation of CD36 mRNA expression as the pathways via which *P. lentiscus* triterpenes exert antioxidant/antiatherogenic effect.

Antimicrobial activity: In vitro study antimicrobial activity of *P.lentiscus* extracts was determined both against bacteria (Sarcina lutea, staphylococcus aureus and E.coli) and fungi (Candida albicans, Candida parapsilosis and Torulopis glabrata). Among different plant extractions, decoctions showed the best antimicrobial activity.

Anti-inflammatory activity: Angelike triantafyllou et al reported that mastic gum inhibits PKC which attenuates production of superoxide and H_2O_2 by NADPH oxidases. This antioxidant property has direct implication to the anti-inflammatory activity of the mastic gum.

Antioxidant activity: In a laboratory study the seasonal variation of the essential oil composition, the antioxidant activity and the total phenolic content of *Pistacia lentiscus* L. was investigated. The essential oil composition of *P. lentiscus* L. was characterised by a high monoterpene hydrocarbon fraction (45.0–68.3%), which was found in greater amounts during the flowering stage. At the same stage, the extracts showed the highest free radical-scavenging activity and antioxidant capacity as well as the highest phenolic content.

Anti-helicobacter pylori action: Farhad U Huwez studied anti-helicobacter pylori activity of Mastic in which the H. pylori strains NCTC 11637 and six fresh clinical isolates (three were sensitive and three were resistant to metronidazole) were maintained by passage on 7 percent horse chocolate blood agar at 37°C in a microaerobic atmosphere. Mastic killed the H. pylori NCTC 11637 strain and the six clinical isolates (reduction in the viable count by a factor of 1000) irrespective of the organism's level of susceptibility to nitroimidazoles. The minimal bactericidal concentration at 24 hours for all strains that were studied was 0.06 mg of the crude mastic per millilitre. At lower concentrations, bacterial growth was still significantly inhibited, with a clear post antibiotic effect even at the lowest concentration used, 0.0075 mg per millilitre. These results suggest that mastic has definite antibacterial activity against H. pylori and the anti-peptic-ulcer properties of mastic.

Wound healing effect: In an experimental trial conducted by zouhir djerrou et al, the efficiency of the virgin fatty oil of *Pistacia lentiscus* was assessed for burn wounds healing and concluded that *Pistacia lentiscus* virgin fatty oil promotes significantly wound contraction and reduces epithelialisation period in experimental animals.

Hepatoprotective action: The hepatoprotective effect of the boiled and non-boiled aqueous extracts of *Pistacia lentiscus* was evaluated in vivo using carbon tetrachloride (CCl_4) intoxicated rats. Plant extracts were administrated orally at a dose of

4 ml/kg body weight, containing various amounts of solid matter. Aqueous extract of *P. lentiscus* showed marked hepatoprotective activity against CCl_4 by reducing the activity of the three enzymes viz alkaline phosphatise, alanine aminotransferase and aspartate aminotransferase; and the level of bilirubin. The effect of the non-boiled aqueous extract was more pronounced than that of the boiled extract.

Asgandh

Withania somnifera commonly known as Asgandh or Ashvaganadha is one of the most potent aphrodisiacs used in traditional systems of medicine like Unani medicine and Ayurveda. It is distributed throughout the dried and subtropical parts of India. It grows upto a height of 2–3 ft (about 1 m). Root and leaves are used for medicinal purposes. The root contains several alkaloids including withanine, withananine, withananinine, pseudo-withanine, somnine, somniferine, somniferinine. The leaves of Indian chemotype contain 12 withanolides, including withaferin A. Steroidal lactones of withanolide series have been also isolated from it. Apart from its aphrodisiac activity it has been used for a number disease ailments like scrofula, rheumatism, anxiety neurosis generalized weakness, inflammation, and ulcers, due to its anti-inflammatory, hypnotic, hepatoprotective, antibacterial, diuretic, antiarthritic, sedative narcotic and deobstruent properties without any known side effects. Its aphrodisiac properties have been also found effective in diabetics, also proved effective in improving semen quality as well as in development of testicles on modern scientific parameters by a number of studies of this era.

Botanical name: *Withania somnifera*

Family: Solanaceae

Vernacular names

Urdu: Asgandh, Asgand Nagori

English: Winter cherry Indian ginseng

Arabic: Kakanj Hindi

Persian: Asgandh Nagori, Kaknja-e-Hindi

Assamese: Asgvagandha

Bengali: Ashvagandha, Asvagandha

Gujarati: Asgandha, Asundha, Asana, Ghodakun, Asoda, Asan

Kannada: Angarberu, Hirenaddina-Hire-gadday, Hiremaddina-Gadday, Virenaddlinagadda

Kashmiri: Asgandha   Malayala m Amukkram, Pevette

Marathi: Asagandha, Askagandha, Askandhatilli Askandha, Kanchuki

Oriya: Asugandha

Punjabi: Asgandh, Isgand, Asgandnagar, Aksan

Sanskrit: Ashvaganadha,   Gandhrapatri, Palashaparni, Varahapatri

Tamil: Amukkaram kizargu Amukkuran, Kilangee, Amukkira, Ashuvagandhi

Telegu: Pennerugadda, Asvagandhi, Penneru, Penneroogadda

HABITAT

It is found in Northern Africa, the Mediterranean and the Middle East. It is distributed throughout the drier and subtropical parts of India. 1

BOTANICAL DESCRIPTION

Macroscopic: The plant grows to a height of 2–3 ft (about 1 m). Stems and branches are covered with minute star shaped hairs. Leaves are oval and about 10 cm in length. Flowers are greenish yellow, borne in axillary clusters. Fruits are smooth red, raisin-sized. The roots are straight, unbranched, thickness varying with age, roots bear fiber like secondary roots, outer surface buff to grey-yellow with longitudinal wrinkles; crown consists of 2-6 remains of stem base; stem bases variously thicked; nodes prominent only on the side from where petiole arises, cylindrical, green with longitudinal wrinkles fracture, short and uneven; odour characterstic; taste bitter and acrid.

Microscopic: The transverse section of root shows cork exfoliated or crushed; when present isodiamatric and nonlignified; cork cambium of 2-4 diffused rows of cells; secondary cortex about twenty layers of compact parenchymatous cells; phloem consists of sieve tubes companion cells, phloem parenchyma; cambium 4-5 rows of tangentially elongated cells; secondary xylem hard forming a closed vascular ring separated by multiseriate medullary rays; a few xylem parenchyma.

Dosage: 5 to 10 gram

Action mentioned in Unani medicine

Mohallile Warm (Anti-inflammatory), Muqawwie Aam (General tonic), Muqawwie Meda (Stomachic), Muwallide Mani (Semenogogue), ,Musammine Badan, Musakkine Asab (Nervine tonic), Munawwim (Sedative), Muaqwwie Bah (Aphrodisiac), Muaqwwie Rahm, Mufattite hisat (Lithotriptic) Mudammile quruh (Ulcer healing), Muqawwie hafiza , Musaffie dam (Blood purifier), Mughallize mani, Muwallide Sheer (Galactogogue).

Uses mentioned in Unani medicine

Sailanur Rahem (Leucorrhoea), Jiryan (Spermatorrhoea), Riqqate Mani, Wajul Qutn (Lumabago), Wajul Mafasil (Arthritis), Zofe

Bah(Sexual weakness), Ghatiya (Rheumatism) Bars(Vitiligo) Taoon (Plague), Bawaseere damwi (Bleeding piles), Warame Khussiya (Orchitis), Hisate gurda wa masana (Kidney and bladder calculi), Nisyan (Amnesia), Qillate mani (oligospermia).

IMPORTANT FORMULATIONS Majoone Sohag, Majoone Salab, Zimade Mohallil, Kushtae Gaodanti.

Side effects No side effects have been reported with Asgandh.

ETHNOBOTANICAL DESCRIPTION

Action Anti-inflammatory, alterative, aphrodisiac, sedative, hypnotic, hepatoprotective, antibacterial, , diuretic, , antitumour, antiarthritic, tonic sedative narcotic deobstruent.

 Uses

Tumours, sexual weakness, scrofula, rheumatism, , anxiety neurosis, generalized weakness, inflammations, ulcers, spermatorhhoea.

CHEMICAL CONSTITUENTS

The root contains several alkaloids, including withanine, withananine, withananinine, pseudo-withanine, somnine, somniferine, somniferinine. The leaves of Indian chemotype contain 12 withanolides, including withaferin A. Steroidal lactones of withanolide series have been isolated. Withanine is sedative and hypnotic. Withaferin A is antitumour, antiarthritic and antibacterial. Anti-inflammatory activity has been attributed to biologically active steroids, of which withaferin A is a major component. The activity is comparable to that of hydrocortisone sodium succinate. Withaferin A also showed significantly protective effect against CCl4 induced hepatotoxicity in rats. The root extract contains an ingredient which has GABA mimetic activity. The free amino acids present in the root include aspartic acid, glycine, tyrosine, alanine, proline, tryptophan, glutamic acid and cystine. The total alkaloids of the root exhibited prolonged hypotensive, bradycardiac and depressant action of the higher cerebral centres in several experimental animals. A withanolide-free aqueous fraction isolated from the roots of Withania somnifera exhibited antistress activity in a dose-dependent manner in mice.

SCIENTIFIC REPORTS

Anti-stress activity A study was performed to understand the role of stress in male infertility, and to test the ability of W. somnifera to combat stress and treat male infertility. Researchers had selected normozoospermic but infertile individuals (n = 60). Normozoospermic fertile men (n = 60) were recruited as controls. The subjects were given root powder of W. somnifera 5 g/day for 3months. They measured various biochemical and stress parameters before and after treatment, suggested a definite role of stress in male infertility and the ability of W. Somnifera to treat stressrelated infertility. Treatment resulted in a decrease in stress, improved the level of anti-oxidants and improved overall semen quality in a significant number of individuals. The treatment resulted in pregnancy in the partners of 14% of the patients.

Testicular development Abdel Magied EM et al in a study at evaluated the effect of lyophilized aqueous extract of Cynomorium coccineum and Withania somnifera on testicular development and on serum levels of testosterone, ICSH and FSH in immature male Wistar rats. There was a notable increase in testicular weight of animals treated with both extracts. Histological examination revealed an apparent increase in the diameter of seminiferous tubules and the number of seminiferous tubular cell layers in the testes of treated rats as compared with control ones.

Thyroid dysfunction The effects of daily administration of Withania somnifera root extract (1.4 g/kg body wt.) and Bauhinia purpurea bark extracts (2.5 mg/kg body wt.) for 20 days on thyroid function in female mice were investigated. It was reported that serum tri-iodothyronine (T3) and thyroxine (T4) concentrations were increased significantly by bauhinia, withania could enhance only serum T4 concentration.

Appetizer activity In a study alcoholic extracts of Withania somnifera was administered for 21 days in stress induced anorexic rats and LPS-induced anorexic rats. The results of study showed that alcoholic root extract of Withania somnifera (100 and 300 mg/kg) dose dependently increases food consumption, number of attempts for food consumption and body weight in stress induced anorexic rats and LPS induced anorexic rats.

Anthelminthic activity Shukla Kirtiman et al was tested the hydroalcoholic extracts of Withania sominifera against adult Pheretima posthuma worms for the evaluation of anthelmintic activity at various concentrations. The results were expressed in terms of time for paralysis and time for death of worms. They showed that the extract exhibited significant wormicidal activity at dose of 40 mg/ml.

Antidepressant activity

Jayanthi MK et al carried out an experimental study using 3 models, behavioural despair tests, forced swim test (FST), tail suspension test (TST) and anti-reserpine test. Effect of different doses of Asgandh was studied on behavioural despair tests induced immobility time and reserpine antagonism. It produced dose dependent decrease in immobility time in chronic studies in FST and TST model, maximum effect being observed with the dose 40 mg/kg.

Anti microbial activity

The study conducted by Premlata Singariya et al shows antimicrobial property of Withania somnifera, in this study the crude extracts of Withania somnifera were successively extracted with polar to non polar solvents using soxhlet assembly. The extracts were then screened for their antimicrobial activity in-vitro against one gram positive bacteria (Bacillus subtilis), two gram negative bacteria (Pseudomonas aeruginosa and Enterobactor aerogens) and one fungus (Aspergillus flavus) by disc diffusion assay. Serial dilution method was used to determine minimum inhibitory concentration (MIC) and minimum bactericidal/fungicidal concentration. The chloroform extract of calyx of Withania somnifera showed highest activity against B. Subtilis.

Chondroprotective activity Venil N et al in a study on explant model of human osteoarthritis cartilage found that W. Somnifera root powders showed reproducible, statistically significant, shortterm chondroprotective activity in 50% of osteoarthritis cases tested in an explant model of human osteoarthritis cartilage damage.

Cardioproptective A study conducted by Das PK et al suggests that the constituents of Withania somnifera are structurally similar to digoxin are demonstrated exhibit cardiotonic activity and provide a salutary effect in CHF. 19 Positive inotropic activity In a study conducted Withania somnifera has been reported to have autonomic ganglion blocking action and myocardial depressant effects and reduce blood pressure due to its positive inotropic and chronotropic Properties.

Activity in Inflammatory bowel disease (IBD) A study based on concentration dependant antioxidant activity of the extracts of Withania somnifera was carried out and results were evaluated using biochemical assays like, inhibition of lipid peroxidation, no scavenging, H_2O_2 scavenging, and ferric reducing power assay. This study supported antioxidant potential of aqueous extract of roots of Withania somnifera and it's utility to ameliorate inflammation, which is the key pathology in inflammatory bowel disease (IBD). The topical application in the form of rectal gel formulation proved to be as effective as the mesalamine treatment.

Anti hypertensive activity

Malhotra CL et al in a study to find antihypertensive effects of Asgandh revealed that the alkaloids had a prolonged hypotensive, bradycardiac and respiratory-stimulant actions.

.Anti diabetic properties A clinical trial was conducted to assess antidiabetic activity of poly-herbal formulation containing Withania somnifera. It was concluded that the formulation was efficient in reducing higher sugar level, potentiating the immune system and improving the anti-oxidant status of diabetic patients.

Osteoarhiritis

Kulkarni RR et al in a double blind study revealed the clinical efficacy of a herbomineral formulation containing roots of Withania somnifera. The results showed that treatment with the herbomineral formulation produced a significant drop in severity of pain and disability score. Radiological assessment, however, did not show any significant changes in both the groups.

Analgesic activity

Twajj et al in a study stated the analgesic effects of Asgandh that soothes nervous system from pain response and hence used as potent analgesic in traditional system of medicine.

Hypothyroidism

Studies on animal models revealed Asgandh has a thyrotropic effect. An aqueous extract of dried withania root was given to mice via gastric intubation at a dose of 1.4 g/kg body weight daily for 20 days. Serum was collected at the end of the 20 day period and analyzed for T3 and T4 concentrations and lipid peroxidation was measured in liver homogenate via antioxidant enzyme activity. Significant increases in serum T4 were observed, indicating the plant has a stimulatory effect at the glandular level.

SATAVAR

Satavar is a well known drug of plant origin which belongs to the family Liliaceae. It is a native of Europe and has been in cultivation for over 2000 years. It is a favorite spring vegetable of the Greeks and Romans. It is found throughout tropical and subtropical parts of India up to an altitude of 1500 m and also distributed in Bangladesh, Africa, Jawa, Australia and Pakistan. It is a perennial shrub which appears in October, while its roots and young shoots are used for medicinal purposes, its young spears are consumed as vegetable or salad and are considered as a balanced health food with many essential nutrients. Black, well drained and fertile soil is good for its cultivation, but can also be cultivated in loose and medium black soil. It is cultivated in gardens as a potted plant for its graceful feathery leaves and flowers. The roots contain long needle shaped structure known as pith which is meant for the conduction of water. It is mainly known for its phytoestrogenic properties. Chemical analysis of Satavar reveals that it contains alkaloids, steroids, saponins, carbohydrates and mucilages. It has been used in Indian traditional systems of medicine mainly in Ayurveda and Unani Tibb since centuries ago as a potent aphrodisiac and galactogogue drug. Recent scientific researchers also support its traditional claims.

Botanical name: *Asparagus racemosus* Willd

Family: Liliaceae

Vernaculars

Unani: Satavar

Urdu: Satavar

Hindi: Satavare, Satawar, Bojhidan, Sadabori

English: Asparagus

Sanskrit: Shatavari, Shatamoolee, Satamuli

Bengali: Satmuli, Satamuli

Tamil: Paniyanaku, Kilavari,

Sindhi: Satwari

Gujrati: Shatawari

Arabic: Shaqaqul

Telugu: Pillitega

 Malayalam: Chatavali, Satavali, Satavari

Marathi: Asvel, Satavarimul

Punjabi: Bozandan, Bozidun

Plant Morphology

It is about 1-2 m long woody, scandent, much-branched, spinous under-shrub with cylindrical, tuberous and fleshy roots and sweet scented white flowers which are unisexual in nature. Spines are sharp and bent. The leaves are 2-6 inches long, reduced to small scales or needlelike spines called cladodes. They are linear, small and arranged in a tuft. Fruits appear in winter which is shiny and red in color. Fruits are small, gram sized, globular or obscurely lobed, pulpy berries which are purplish black when they are ripened, seeds are hard and brittle. The roots are 30-100 cm in length and 1-2 cm in thickness and found in clusters. These finger like roots are soft and pliable. They are silvery white or ash colored externally and white internally. They are mucilaginous and somewhat sweet in taste.

Parts Used Root tubers and leaves

Dosage 7-10 gm; 12-15 gm; 5-7 gm. (powder of roots)

Action mentioned in Unani system of Medicine

In classical Unani literature, following important therapeutic actions of Asparagus recemosus are mentioned. Muqawwie bah (aphrodisiac), Mughallize mani, Mudire labn(galactogogue), Musakhhine meda, Qatae balgham, Musakkin (Analgesic), Mugharri (Demulscent), Muqawwie rehm (Uterine tonic), Mohallile warm (Anti-inflammatory), Muallide mani (Semenogogue), and Muqawwie qalb (Cardiac tonic).

Medicinal Uses

The important therapeutic uses of Satavar described in classic Unani texts are given below. It is useful in bawaseer (hemorrhoids), amraze chashm (Eye diorders),sozishe bol(Burning micturition), jiryan (Spermatorrhoea), riqqate mani, fasaade khoon, waja ul mafasil(Arthritis), juzam (Leprosy), Diq (tuberculosis), Suaal (cough), Zoafe aam (debility), isahal(Diarrhoea) and pechish (Dysentery).

- Juice of root with honey is effective in sailane rehm (leucorrhoea).
- Powder of root with milk is used to improve breast milk production.

- Juice of fresh roots is useful for the patients of Suzak (Gonorrhoea).

- Decoction or powder of its Root acts as a general tonic and also indicated in sexual debility.

The boiled cladodes are applied externally for suppression of boils and tumours.

Ethnobotanical Actions

Ethnobotanical review of literature of Asperagus recemosus reveals that it possesses following important actions. Demulcent, Diuretic, Aphrodisiac, Galactogogue, Refrigerant, Anti spasmodic, Alterative tonic, Amebicide, Anticancer, Anti-inflammatory, Antipyretic, Styptic, and Immunomodulator.

Ethnobotanical Uses

It is employed in diarrhoea as well as in cases of colic and dysentery.

- The root is boiled in milk and it is administered to relieve bilious dyspepsia and diarrhoea and to promote appetite.

- The tubers are candied and taken as a sweetmeat.

- The fresh root juice is given with honey as a demulcent.

- The boiled leaves smeared with ghee are applied to boils, small pox etc.

- The roots along with the leaves of Gymnema sylvestre are given in diabetes.

- Oil of the root is recommended in the treatment of rheumatism and nervine disorders.

SCIETIFIC PROVEN COMPOUND DRUGS FOR OLIGOSPERMIA

Majoone bhangra 5grams twice a day

- Halwae supari pak 6 grams twice a day
- Safoofe sailanur rehm 5 grams twice a day with milk
- Safoofe salab 5 grams twice a day
- Safoofe shahi khas 3 grams twice a day

Phytochemistry

The asparagus roots contain alkaloids, triterpenoids, steroids, saponins, carbohydrates, lactones, flavonides (kaempferol, quercetin, and rutin), glycosides and mucilages.The mineral constituents of the root are: calcium 0.172; copper 0.033; sodium 14.60; potassium 8.32; magnesium 0.169; manganese 0.0074; nickel 0.105and zinc 0.072 mg/g20 and traces of phosphorus and iron. The glycosides present in the root are shatavarins I-V,20,24 n-butyl-beta-Dfructopyranoside, glycoside-AR-4,24 tridecaacetyl shatavarin I, tetradeca-O-methylshatavarin I, sarsasapogenin, immunoside.

The ethanolic extract of roots of the plant is reported to yield a polycyclic alkaloid, asparagamine. Its leaves contain diosgenin and quercetin-3 glucuronide while flowers and fruits contain quercetin, rutin and hyperoside. This plant also contains vitamin A, B1, B2, C, E, and folic acid. Other chemical constituents of asparagus are essential oils, asparagines, arginine, tyrosine, resin, and tannin.

SCIENTIFIC REPORTS

Wound healing activity: Prabhath et al conducted a study on albino rats to prove wound healing effect of satavar. They administered aqueous extract of the root of Asparagus racemosus in a dose of 200mg/kg and 400mg/kg orally for 10 to 22 days in 12 week old healthy male Wistar rats weighing 150-250 g. It increased the level of IL-1 and TNF resulting in stimulation of fibroblast and collagenase activity, thus helping in wound healing as well as wound remodeling.

Hepatoprotective activity: A study was conducted on male albino rats of Wistar strain proved its hepatoprotective activity. Rats with body weight of 160-180 g were treated with A. racemosus extract (50mg/kg) for 21 days. It has been observed that A. racemosus extract prevented isoniazid-induced hepatotoxicity by inhibiting the production of free radicals via inhibition of hepatic CYP2E1 activity and increasing the removal of free radicals through the induction of antioxidant enzymes.

Memory enhancing activity: Memory deficit (amnesia) was induced in Swiss albino male mice by administration of scopolamine and sodium nitrite intraperitoneally. Methanolic roots extract of Asparagus racemosus prevented experimental amnesia and it may be a great potential in memory deficit.

Antibacterial activity: K. Ravishankar et al in their study confirmed that ethanolic extract of root of Asparagus racemosus has antibacterial activity against Staphylococcus aureus, Bacillus subtilis, Staphylococcus werneri, Pseudomonas putida,

Pseudomonas aeruginosa, Proteus mirabilis etc, which may be attributed to presence of different phyto-constituents like alkaloids, phenolic compounds, saponins and flavonoids etc.

Nutritional effects: Kumari et al investigated the nutritional effects of herbal preparation of Asparagus racemosus in 50 day old broiler chicks. The results were encouraging in relation to total body weight and feed conversion efficiency. The researchers found that it can also be used potentially before mass vaccination of the chicks for its property of immune-modulation like levamisole.

Anti hyperglycemic activity: The ethanolic extracts, of roots of Asparagus racemosus stimulates insulin secretion and contributes to anti hyperglycemic action. Lipid lowering and antioxidant property: It has been reported that Asparagus racemosus root powder administration decreases plasma lipids and oxidative stress in hyperlipidemic conditions which were produced by administration of cholesterol and bile salt in diet in male albino rats.

Galactogogue activity: A clinical trial was conducted in 60 lactating mothers showed that Asparagus racemosus has significant galactogogue activity in comparison with the placebo control group without any significant acute toxic effects.

Aphrodisiac activity: A study was carried out on adult albino rats suggested that the systemic use of extracts of Satavar has sexual behavior enhancing effect in male rats. A single dose of 3000mg/kg was administered that was found to stimulate the mounting behavior of male rat and also increase their mating performance. No general short term toxicity was noticed.

Anti-depressent activity: Dhingra and Kumar in their study concluded that methanolic extract of Asparagus racemosus showed significant antidepressant activity probably by inhibiting MAO-A and MAO-B; and through interaction with adrenergic, dopaminergic, serotonergic and GABAergic systems.

Laboob Kabeer Khaas

1. Khashkhash Safaid   290 g
2. Mahi Roobian   150 g
3. Khulanjan   150 g
4. Shaqaq-ul-Misri   300 g
5. Beheman Safaid   150 g
6. Beheman Surkh   150 g
7. Tudri Zard   150 g
8. Tudri Safaid   150 g
9. Zanjabeel Khushk   150 g
10. Kunjad Safaid Muqash-shar 150 g
11. Dar-e-Filfil   80 g
12. Suranjan Shireen   110 g
13. Buzidan   110g
14. Pudina Khushk   110 g
15. Sumbul-ut-Teeb   80 g
16. Sad Kufi   80 g
17. Kababchini   80 g
18. Inderjao Shireen   80 g
19. Darunaj Aqrabi   80 g
20. Zarawand Mudharaj   80 g
21. Anar Dana   80 g
22. Tukhm-e-Gazar   80 g
23. Maghz-e-Pambadana   150g
24. Tukhm-e-Turb   80 g
25. Tukhm-e-Shaljam   80 g
26. Tukhm-e-Piyaz   80 g
27. Tukhm-e-Shibat   80 g
28. Ushna (Chadila)   60 g
29. Ood Kham   70 g
30. Narjeel Giri   290 g
31. Maghz-e-Badam Shireen   150 g
32. Maghz-e-Pista   150 g

33. Maghz-e-Akhrot	150 g
34. Darchini	150 g
35. Jaifal	120 g
36. Qaranfal Guldar	80 g
37. Maghz-e-Chironji	150 g
38. Maghz-e-Tarbuz	150 g
39. Mastagi Roomi	100 g
40. Salab Gatta	290 g
41. Maghz-e-Funduq	150 g
42. Araq-e-Kewra	562 ml
43. Qand Safaid	22.50 Kg
44. Beer Bahuti	10g
45. Ilaichi Khurd	80 g
46. Zafran	80 g
47. Salajeet	80 g

ACTION: Muqawwi-e-Bah, Muqawwi-e-Aza-e-Raeesa, Muqawwi-e-Qalb, Muqawwi-e-Dimagh, Muqawwie-Kulya, Muqawwi-e-Masana, Muqawwi-e-Asab, Muwallid-e-Mani, Mughalliz-e-Mani

THERAPEUTIC USE: Zof-e-Bah, Zof-e-Aam, Zof-e-Asab, Zof-e-Qalb, Zof-e-Dimagh, Zof-e-Kulya, Zof-e-Masana, Qillate-Mani, Riqqat-e-Mani

DOSE: 6 g with 60 ml Maullaham Khaas or milk once a day

Majun Pumba Dana

1. Shaqaq-ul-Misri   100 g
2. Maghz-e-Binola   190 g
3. Darchini 140 g
4. Tukhm-e-Utangan   140 g
5. Qaranfal Guldar   140 g
6. Zanjabeel   90 g
7. Kaifal   90 g
8. Qust Shireen   40 g
9. Tukhm-e-Katan Biryan   40 g
10. Mastagi Roomi   40 g
11. Behman Surkh   40 g
12. Salab Misri   40 g
13. Musli Safaid   40 g
14. Tukhm-e-Shaljam   40 g
15. Qand Safaid   4 Kg

ACTION: Muqawwi-e-Bah, Muwallid-e-Mani

THERAPEUTIC USE: Riqqat-e-Mani, Jiryan

DOSE: 6 g twice a day

Johar khusiya (Goat Testicles)

1. Bakrey ke khusiye   1Kg
2. Namak sambhar   35 g

THERAPEUTIC USE: Zof-e-Bah, Qillate-Mani,

Riqqat-e-Mani

Dose : 1gm with milk

Majoon Salab

1. Mushk   1.75g
2. Jund Baidastar   3.5g
3. Daronaj aqarabi   3.5g
4. Warq Nuqra   3.5g
5.   Ambar   3.5g
6. Sumbultteeb   5.25g
7. Ilaichi Kalan   5.25g
8. Ood Kham   5.25g
9. Kazmazij   5.25g
10. Smagh Arbi   5.25g
11. Paneer maya Shatr Airabi   7g
12. Barg e Gaozaban   7g
13. Badranjboya   7g
14. Faranjmushk   7g
15. Reeg Mahi   7g
16. Maghz sar kanjzshk nar   7g
17. Maghz Habussanobar   7g
18. Maghz Narjeel   7g
19. Maghz Badam Shireen   7g
20. Maghz Pista   7g
21. Maghz Fundq   7g
22. Bozeedan   10.5g

23. Sooranjan Shireen	10.5g
24. Tudri Surkh	10.5g
25. Tudri Zard	10.5g
26. Bahman Safaid	10.5g
27. Zanjabeel	10.5g
28. Podeena Khusk	10.5g
29. Khask Murbba	10.5g
30. Dana Khashkhash Safaid	10.5g
31. Kanjud Muqashar	10.5g
32. Tukhm Gazar	10.5g
33. Dar e Filfil	10.5g
34. Indarjoshireen	14g
35. Darcheeni	14g
36. Qaranfal	14g
37. Ilaichi Khurd	14g
38. Khulanjan	18g
39. Shaqaqul Misri	18g
40. Kasiyatus Salab	18g
41. Bazrabanj	18g

THERAPEUTIC USE: Zof-e-Bah, Qillate-Mani, Riqqaṭ-e-Mani, Muqawwi Asab, Jiryan Mani

Dose : 7 to 12 gm with milk

APHRODISIACS USED IN UNANI SYSTEM OF MEDICINE

The word aphrodisiac is derived from the name of the Greek goddess of sexual love and beauty, Aphrodite.1 Anaphrodisiac is defined as any food or drug that arouses thesexual instinct, induces venereal desire and increases pleasureand performance. Many natural substances have historicallybeen known as aphrodisiacs in Africa and Europe, such asYohimbine and the Mandrake plant, as well as groundRhinoceros horn in the Chinese culture and Spanish fly.There are two main types of aphrodisiacs,psychophysiological stimuli (visual, tactile, olfactory andaural) preparations and internal preparations (food, alcoholic drinks and drugs). Sexual relationships are one of the mostimportant social and biological relationships in human life.

The purpose of intercourse is to reproduce and to continuethe process of generation, passion and pleasure form anintegral part of this function. Loss of firm erections is often extremely bothersome to men. Male sexual weakness is termed as impotence which is defined as the persistent failure to develop and maintain erections of sufficient rigidity for penetrative sexual intercourse. Nowadays for impotence the more specific term 'Erectile dysfunction' is preferred. The condition of erectile dysfunction is more common in middle aged population. As per Massachusetts Male Aging Study, the prevalence of erectile dysfunction among the individuals of 40-70 years is 52 %. The incidence of erectile dysfunction is also higher among men with certain medical disorders such as diabetes mellitus, heart disease, hypertension and decreased HDL levels. Smoking is a significant risk factor in the development of erectile dysfunction. Medications used to treat diabetes or cardiovascular diseases are additional risk factors. There is a higher incidence of erectile dysfunction among men who have undergone radiation or surgery for prostate cancer and in those with a lower spinal cord injury. Psychological causes of erectile dysfunction include depression, anger, stress or other causes. Treatment of erectile dysfunction involves local use of vasoactive drugs like papaverine and alprostadin8 and first line oral therapy includes phosphodiesterase type-5 inhibitors such as sildenafil and verdenafil which inhibit hydrolysis of second messenger cyclic guanosine mono phosphate release within penile smooth cells. These drugs have limited efficacy, various side effects and contraindications in certain disease conditions. Sildenafil citrate (Viagra) is a successful drug that modifies the heamodynamics in the penis but these drugs have side effects like headache, flushing, priapism, dyspepsia and nasal congestion. Unani system of medicine is one of the very well organised systems of medicine; it treats sexual problems as a separate and integral part of medical science. Every aspect of sexuality from sexual debility to venereal diseases is discussed in details. Classical Unani medical literature has given much importance to sexual debility or impotency. Avicenna has a totally different approach in the diagnosis, selection and administration of drugs in treating sexual debility and improving sexual performance. As per his view the three vital organs viz liver, heart and brain control the genital organs. Liver supplies the pure blood to the genitals, heart provides required heat and the Brain provides the power of senses. A number of Muqawwie bah drugs (Aphrodisiac) are mentioned below which have been in use by ancient Unani physicians since centuries for the management of various sexual disorders. These drugs are time tested safe and effective.

S. No.	Botanical Name	Unani Name	Parts Used
1	*Abelmoschus esculantus* (L.)	Bamiya	**Fruits**
2	*Abrus precatorius* L.	Ghongchi	**Seed**
3	*Acacia Arabica* Willd.	Samaghe arabi	**Gum**
4	*Aconitum heterophyllum* Wall.	Atees	**Root**
5	*Aconitumn apellus*	Beesh	**Root**
6	*Acorus calamus* Linn.	Waj turkey	**Root**
7	*Allium sativum* L.	Soom/Lehsun	**Bulb**
8	*Allium cepa* L.	Piyaz	**Bulb**
9	*Alpiniaga langa* Willd.	Khulanjan	**Root**
10	*Anacyclu spyrethrum* DC.	Aqarqarha	**Root**
11	*Asaru meuropaeum* Linn.	Asaroon	**Root**
12	*Asparagusrac emosus* Willd.	Satawar	**Root**
13	*Aristolochia rotunda*	Zaravand	**Root**
14	*Asteracantha longifolia*	Talmakhana	**Seed**

15	*Bacopa monnieri* L.	Brahmi	**Whole plant**
16	*Blepharis edulis* Linn.	Tukhme Anjra	**Seed**
17	*Boswellia serrata*	Kundoor	**Gum**
18	*Brassica rapa*	Tukhme Shaljam	**Seed**
19	*Buchanania latifolia* Roxb.	Chironji	**Fruit**
20	*Butea frondosa* Roxb.	Dhak	**Gum**
21	*Cannabis indica* L.	Qinnab	**Leaf**
22	*Capsicum annuum* L.	Filfil	**Seed**
23	*Carica papaya* L.	Papita	**Fruit**
24	*Celastrus paniculatus*	Malkangani	**Seed**
25	*Centaurea behen*	Behman Safaid	**Root**
26	*Ceratonia siliqua* Linn	Kharnoob	**Seed**
27	*Cicer arietinum*	Nakhud	**Seed**
28	*Cinnamomum aromaticum*	Taj	**Bark**
29	*Cinnamomum zeylanicum*	Darchini	**Bark**
30	*Cheiranthus cheiri*	Tudrizard	**Seed**
31	*Chlorophytum arundinaceum*	Muslisafaid	**Root**
32	*Cochlospermum religiosum*	Kateera	**Gum**
33	*Commiphora mukul* Hook.exStocks	Muqil	**Gum**
34	*Commiphora myrrha*	Mur	**Resin**
35	*Cocos nucifera*Linn.	Narjeel	**Endosperm**
36	*Corulus avellana*	Funduq	**Fruit**
37	*Crocus sativus*Linn.	Zaafran	**Stigma**
38	*Cucumis melo*Linn.	Kharpaza	**Seed**
39	*Curculigo orchioides*	Musli siyah	**Root**
40	*Curcuma amada*Roxb.	Amba haldi	**Rhizome**
41	*Curcuma zedouria*Rosc.	Zaranbad	**Rhizome**
42	*Daucus carota*L.	Gazar	**Root**
43	*Dolichos lablab*Linn	Lobia	**Seed**
44	*Elettaria cardamomum*	Qaqla	**Fruits**
45	*Euphorbia hirta*L.	Dudhi	**Leaves**
46	*Euphorbia royleana*	Sheere thuhar	**Resin**

47	*Eruca sativa* Mill.	Jarjeer	**Seed**
48	*Ferula foetida*	Hilteet	**Resin**
49	*Ficus carica*	Injeer	**Fruits**
50	*Ficus religiosa* Linn.	Bargad	**Leaves**
51	*Gossypium herbaceum* Linn	Pambadana	**Seed**
52	*Glycyrrhiza glabra*Linn.	Aslasoos	**Root**
53	*Hibiscus rosa-sinesis*	Gurhal	**Flower**
54	*Lactuca scariola*	Tukhme kahu	**Seed**
55	*Lepidium sativum*	Halyoon	**Seed**
56	*Lapinus albus*	Turmus	**Seed**
57	*Linum usitatissimum*	Katan	**Seed**
58	*Mathiola incana*	Tudri surkh	**Seed**
59	*Melia azedarach*	Bakain	**Seed**
60	*Mentha arvensis*Linn	Nana	**Whole plant**
61	*Moschusmoschiferus*	Mushk	**Glands secretion**
62	*Myristica fragrans*	Jaiphal	**Fruit**
63	*Mangifera indica*L.	Aam	**Fruit**
64	*Mucuna pruriens* Linn. DC.	Konch	**Seed**
65	*Nerium odorum*Aiton	Kharzohra	**Leaf, Root**
66	*Orchis latifolia*Linn.	Salab misri	**Root**
67	*Pastinaca secacul*	Shaqaqul misri	**Root**
68	*Peganum harmala*	Aspand	**Seed**
69	*Phoenix dactylifera*	Khurma	**Fruits**
70	*Pinus longifolia* Roxb.	Sanober	**Pine nut**
71	*Pipe rlongum*	Filfil daraz	**Fruits**
72	*Pistacia vera* Linn.	Pista	**Fruit**
73	*Prunus amygdalus*	Badam	**Fruits**
74	*Pyrethrum indicum*DC	Bozidan	**Root**
75	*Raphanus sativus* Linn.	Turb	**Seed**
76	*Rauwolfia serpentine*	Asrol	**Root**
77	*Ricinus communis* L.	Bed anjir	**Seed**
78	*Rosa damascena*Mill	Gule surkh	**Petal**
79	*Salmaliamalabarica*	Sembhal	**Root, Gum**
80	*Salvia hae matodes*	Behman surkh	**Root**

81	*Saussurea lappa*	Kusht shirin	**Root**
82	*Semecarpus anacardium*	Biladur	**Fruit**
83	*Sesamumind icum* Linn.	Kunjad	**Seed**
84	*Sida cordifolia*	Beejband	**Seed**
85	*Sphaeranthus indicus* Linn.	Mundi	**Whole plant**
86	*Symplocos racemosus*	Lodh pathani	**Bark**
87	*Strychnosnux-vomica*Linn.	Azaraqi	**Seeds**
88	*Syzygiumarom aticum*L.	Qaranfal	**Driedfl owerbu ds**
89	*Tamarindus indica* L.	Tamarhindi	**Seed**
90	*Trapa bispinosa*	Sighara	**Fruit**
91	*Tribulus terrestris* L.	Kharkhasak	**Whole plant**
92	*Withania somnifera* Linn.	Asgandh	**Root**
93	*Trigonella foenum-graecum*	Methi	**Seed**
94	*Vitis vinifera*	Kishmish	**Fruit**
95	*Wrightia tinctoria* (Roxb.)	Indarjao	**Seed**
96	*Zingiber officinale*Roscoe	Zanjabeel	**Rhizome**

Jima (Sexual Intercourse) - in the Light of Legend *Greek-Arab* Philosophers with Special References

Jima (coitus) is act by which, Semen is to be expelled out of the body because; it retains in the body for long period, will lead to fatal diseases. Its elimination is a natural process through the natural act. Greek philosophers said that the *Jima* affects the body according to temperament of being. Some directives, advantages and disadvantages about *Jima* have been delivered by renowned Unani physicians thousands of year back.

ALLAMA IBN-UL-QAIEM AL JOZI- (TIB NABVI)

Aim of jima- There are three aims of *Jima First-* For existence of humanity. *Second-* Elimination of semen, because it retains more, causes disease.

Third- To overcome of sexual desire and feeling of well fullness.

Retention of semen leads to fatal diseases like *Janun* and *Mirgi* (epilepsy) etc. To avert these problems, Tabiyat (natural power of the body) eliminates semen with the help of *Ehtelam* (night fall). Mohd Bin Zakaria Razi stated that away from Jima for long time, is the leading cause for weakness of nervous system, *Suddah* (blockage) develops in the seminal passages, coldness of body and movement restricted, loss of sexual desire and disturbed digestion.

- After *Jima* we should take Wazu or Taharat or bath, which increases the pleasure with the heart because Hazrat Mohammad (PBUH) takes *Taharat* (bath) between two Jima.

- Best time for *Jima* is after proper digestion of food.

- *Jima* with old women, premature girl, women having loss of libido and diseased women leads to weakness of physical strength in man.

- Position for *Jima* is that, man should be on top.

- The worst position is that, the Women on top. Hazrat Mohammad (PBUH) stated that:

- "به الناس حتى يدخل النارا
حشر يوم القيامه و ريحه انتن من الجيفة يتاذى
من نكح امراءة فى دبرها او رجلا او صبيا"

Meaning of statement- Do not do anal intercourse (*Jima* fil Dubur).

- *Jima* during menstrual bleeding may cause Leprosy.

- Haris Bin Kaldah stated that: on full stomach and *Jima* with senile women annihilate the health. 1

IBN SINA (Avicenna)- AL QANOON FIL TIB (Canon of Medicine)

Advantages-

- Feeling of lightness.

- Enhances the growth of body.

- It releases the stress.

- Sensation of valour and youthfulness.

- Decreases the rage.

- Melancholic patients find relief.

- Beneficial in black bile (Sauda) diseases.

- Gives relief in hyperemic renal pain.

- Phlegmatic diseases become sluggish.

- It acts as an appetizer.

- It minimizes the testicular inflammatory substances.

- Beneficial for aversion, headache and blackout.

- It releases the inflammation of hip joint.

Disadvantages-

- Elimination of nutritional substances.

- Leads to general weakness.

- Produces the coldness and dryness in the body.

- Decreases the Hararat-e-Gharizia (innate energy).

- Leads to tinnitus, weakness of eyesight and hearing.

- Feeling of weakness and pain in calf muscle area.

- Sometime leads to epilepsy.

- Vertigo develops.

- Acute hyperemic fever occurs.

- Tremor and insomnia have been also seen.

- Baldness and dandruff appear.

- Pain in kidney and urinary bladder get increase.

- Constipation and colic pain are also observed.

- Complaint of bad smell from mouth and gums.

- Grumbling in *Zof-e-Hazm* (Indigestion).

- Increases the thoracic pain and stomachache if exist previously.

ZAKARIA RAZI (Razes)- KITAB-UL-MURSHID

Advantages-

- It is beneficial if headache is due to avoidance of *Jima* (intercourse).
- Inflamed testes and ureter because of retention of semen get relief.

Disadvantages-

- The condition of asthmatic patient becomes worst.
- Harmful for *Har Mizaj* (hot temperament) persons.
- It hurts to those who feel weakness after coitus.
- Away from coitus in very hot season.

ALLAMA BURHANUDDIN NAFIS BIN AUZ KIRMANI - KULLIYAT NAFISI

Timing for jima-

- *Jima* after digestion of food is useful.

- Body should be on moderate condition.

- With full desire of sex.

Advantages-

- *Jima* provides happiness and activeness.

- It uplifts the innate energy.

- Makes the organs able to receive the proper nutrition.

- It reduces the anxiety.

- Minimizes the anger and anguish.

- It is beneficial for melancholic and phlegmatic patients.

- Appropriate coitus prevents the vertigo, vision disturbances, inflammation of testicles and ureter also.

Disadvantages-

- Coitus on full stomach leads to digestive problems and formation of impure Akhlat.

- Over *Jima*/frequent coitus produces weakness in the body.

- Due to over activity during coitus dryness and weakness develop.

- Multiple coitus may develop *Rasha* (tremors), *Falij* (paralysis) and tetanic condition.

ZAKARIA RAZI (Razes)- (KITAB UL MANSURI)

Timing for jima and other instructions

- Don't coitus on empty stomach.

- One should away from *Jima* (coitus) just after *Is-hal* (loose motion), *Fasad* (Venesection), *Hijamat* (cupping) and *Qay* (vomiting).

- Take semen producing diet.

- Drinking of concentrated sweet substances after Jima (coitus).

- Take proper sleep also.

Advantages-

- Jima (coitus) makes the body healthy.

- Decreases the obesity.

- Feeling of well fullness.

- Releases the tension.
- It cures the melancholia.
- It also prevents the psychosomatic disorders.

Disadvantages-

- Excess coitus leads to sunken eyes and loss of libido.
- It may cause *Diq* (tuberculosis) in the hot temperament persons.
- Atypical *Jima* produces slimness of the body.

IBN HUBEL BAGHDADI- AL- MUKHTARAT FIL TIB

Best timing for jima and other instructions-

- After proper digestion of food.
- Before appetite and before empty of stomach.
- Best seasons are Rabi (spring) and Sarma (winter).
- Do not perform Jima during anger, stress and fear.
- Away from *Jima* (coitus) after Hammam (hot bath), profound work out and long time illnesses.

- Desist from *Jima* in case of Jiryan-ud-dam (hemorrhage), Bawasir (piles), bleeding diarrhea and Naksir (Epistaxis).

Advantages-

- Feeling of lightness and wellness.

- Buqrat stated that Jima is principle for deterrence of health.

- Proper *Jima* (coitus) provides strength to the testes and seminal vesicle.

- Produces *Harat-e-Gharizia* (innate energy) in the body.

- Refrain from Jima leads to formation of impure semen and vapour which goes to brain and leads to Janun (insanity).

- *Harart-e-Gharizia* (Innate energy) becomes strong.

- Releases the sadness and despair.

Disadvantages-

- Frequent *Jima* causes removal of *Johar-e-Saleha* (useful substances) from body and leads to *Laghri* (thinness).

- In *Barid Yabis* (cold dry) *Mizaj* having persons

- Jima decreases the *Hararat-e-Gharizia* (innate energy).

- Laxity of organs.

- Palpitation.

- Pain in thorax and lungs.

Arthralgia, colic pain and vertigo become most awful.

BIBLIOGRAPHY

1. Walsh Patrick C (Ed.). Campbell's Urology. Vol 2, 8th ed. Saunders publication; 2002: 1488.

2. Mazhar Mushtaq, Saghir Ahmed Jafri, Abdus Salam Sheikh, Sadia Ahmad, Farah Deeba, Khurram Salam. Human Chorionic Gonadotropin (hCG): A treatment of oligospermia. Pak J Med Sci October - December 2007 (Part-II); 23(6): 840-6.

3. Tikkiwal M, Ajmera RL, Mathur NK. Effect of zinc administration on seminal zinc and fertility of oligospermic males. Indian J Physiol Pharmacol Jan-Mar1987; 31(1): 30-4.

4. Smith Roger P. Gynaecology in Primary Care. Williams and Wilkens Publication; 1997: 356.

5. John O Schorge, Joseph I Schaffer, Lisa M Halvorson, Barbara L Hoffman , Karen Bradshaw D and Gary Cunningham F. William's Gynaecology. McGraw Hills Pub; 2008:870-941.

6. Brandon J, Bankowski MD, Amy E, Hearne MD and Nicholas C. The Johns Hopkins Manual of Gynecology and Obstetrics. 2nd ed. Lippincott Williams and Wilkins Publishers; 2002: 157.

7. Jonathan Berek S. Novak's Gynaecology. Lippincott Williams and Wilkins Publishers; 2002: 400-7.

8. Leon Speroff, Robert Glass H and Nathan Kase G. Clinical Gynaecologic Endocrinology and Infertility. 6th ed. Lippincott Williams and Wilkins; 1999: 425.

9. Sengupta Sree Bijoy, Datta DC and Chattopadhyay Sisir K. Gynaecology for Postgraduates and Practitnors. 1st ed. Churchill livingstone; 1998:59-60.

10. Dhaliwal LK, Gupta KR and Majumdar S. Treatment of Oligospermia with Speman: A Formulation of Plant Origin. Indian Medical Gazette 2001 Nov: 375-79.

11. Bashir Ahmed. Mujarrebate Bashir. Lucknow:Raja Ram press ; 1954:22-3.

12. Kabiruddin M. Al Aksir. Vol 2. New Delhi: Ejaz publishing house; YNM: 1255-70.

13. Majusi Ibn Abbas. Kamilus Sina'ah. (Urdu Translation by Kantoori Gulam Hussain). New Delhi: Idara Kitabus Shifa; 2010: 479, 531.

14. Razi Mohammed bin Abubakar Zakariya. Kitabul Hawi. Vol 10th. New Delhi: CCRUM; 2007: 243,281-9,295-7.

15. Ahmed SI. Introduction to Al Umur al Tabi'yah (principles of human physiology in tibb). 1st ed. PNM; 1980: 185-88.

16. Kabeeruddin M. Kulliyate Nafeesi (Urdu translation). New Delhi: Idarae Kitabul Shifa; 1954: 110-14.

17. Abdul Lateef. Qarabadeene Majeedi. 9th ed. New Delhi: All India Unani Tibbi Conference; 1986: 24-28, 43-99, 109-128, 320-399, 410-414.

18. Michael J O' Dowd and Elliot E Philipp. The History of Obstetrics and Gynaecology. London: The Parthenon Publishing group; 2000: 349-69.

19. Spreet H. Iconographia Gyniatrica: A Pictorial History of Gynaecology and Obstetrics. Philadelphia:YNM; 194.

20. Abul Hasan Rabban Tabri. Firdaususl Hikmat (Urdu Translation).New Delhi: Idara Katabul Shifa; 2010: 42-45.

21. Razi Mohammed bin Abubakar Zakariya. Kitabul Mansuri. New Delhi: CCRUM; 1991: 55-56.

22. Ibn Sina. Al Qanoon Fit Tib. (Urdu translation by Kantoori GH).Vol 3rd part 2nd. New Delhi: Idara kitabul shifa; 2007: 1036-9,1050.

23. Ismail Ahmed Hasan Jurjani. Zakhira khwarzam Shahi (Urdu translation by Hadi Hasan khan).Vol.1.New Delhi: Idara kitabul shifa; 2010:110-1.

24. Abu Walid ibn Rushd. Kitabul Kulliyat. New Delhi: CCRUM; 1987: 302.

25. Gruner I and Oskar Cameron T. Al Qanoon fit tibb (English translation). New York: AMS press; 1973: 114-15.

26. Syed Ishtiyaque Ahmed. Kulliyate Asri. Vol 1. New Delhi: New public press; 1983: 175-82.

27. Guyton Arthur C and John E. Text Book of Medical Physiology. 11th ed. Pennsylvania: Elsevier Inc; 2006: 996-1001.

28. Sylvia Mader S. Understanding Human Anatomy and Physiology. 5th ed. The McGraw-Hill Companies; 2004: 343-8.

29. Van De Graaf. Human Anatomy. 6th ed. The McGraw-Hill Companies; 2001: 698-713.

30. Gerard Tortora J and Bryan Derrickson. Principles of anatomy and physiology.12th ed. John Wiley and Sons; 2009: 1082-95.

31. Faller A and Schuenke M. The human body, An Introduction to Structure and Function.13th ed. Germany: Georg Thieme Verlag; 2004: 474-78.

32. Vander, Sherman and luciano. Human Physiology: The mechanisms of body function.9th ed. The McGraw-Hill Companies; 2003: 648-51.

33. Thonneau P, Marchand S, Tallec A, Ferial ML, Ducot B and Lansac J et al. Incidence and main causes of infertility in a resident population (1,850,000) of three French regions. Hum Reprod 1991; 6: 811-16.

34. Leke RJ, Oduma JA, Bassol-Mayagoitia S, Bacha AM and Grigor KM. Regional and

geographical variations in infertility: effects of environmental, cultural, and socioeconomic factor. Environ Health Perspect 1993; 101(2): 73-80.

35. Fisch H and Goluboff ET. Geographic variations in sperm counts: a potential cause of bias in studies of semen quality. Fertil Steril 1996; 65: 1009-14.

36. Auger J and Jouannet P. Evidence for regional differences of semen quality among fertile French men. Federation Francaise des Centres d'Etude et de Conservation des Oeufs et du Sperme humains. Hum Reprod 1997; 12: 740-5.

37. Jorgensen N, Andersen AG, Eustache F, Irvine DS, Suominen J and Petersen JH et al. Regional differences in semen quality in Europe. Hum Reprod 2001; 16: 1012-9.

38. Rajiv Mehta H, Sanjay Makwana, Geetha Ranga M, Srinivasan RJ and Virk SS. Prevalences of oligozoospermia and azoospermia in male partners of infertile couples from different parts of India. Asian J Androl 2006; 8 (1): 89-93.

39. Falcon Tammaso and Falcon Tanya R. The Cleaveland Clinic Guide to Infertility. New York: Kaplan Publishing; 2009: 196.

40. David Warrell A, Timothy Cox M, John Firth D, Edward J and Benz MD. Oxford Text book of Medicine. 4th ed. Oxford Press; 2003: 1272-75.

41. Dohle GR, Colpi GM, Hargreave TB, Papp GK and Jungwirth A et al. EAU Guidelines on Male Infertility. European Urology 2005; vol.48: 703-11.

42. Padubidri VG and Daftary Shirish N. Shaw's Textbook of Gynaecology. 14th ed. Elsevier publication; 2008: 182.

43. Khan Rashid Lateef. Five Teachers Gynaecology. 3rd Ed. CBS Publications; 2003: 264.

44. Lee Goldman and Claude Bennett J. Cecil Textbook of Medicine. 21st ed. WB Saunders Company; 2000: 1379-86.

45. James owen drife. Drugs and sperm. British Medical Journal march 1982; 284: 844-5.

46. Dennis kasper L, Eugene braunwald, Anthony fauci S, Dan longo L and Eugene Braunwald et al. Harrison's principles of internal medicine. McGraw-Hill pub; 2005: 2191-92.

47. Osifo OD and Agbugui JO. Male Infertility Secondary to Varicocele: A Study of the

Management of 45 Patients. Afr J of Reprod Health Apr 2008; 12 (1): 54-9.

48. Khare CP. Indian Medicinal Plants: an Illustrated Dictionary. Berlin: Heidelberg Springer; 2007: 4, 71, 453, 471.

49. Narayan Das Prajapati and Kumar U. Agro's Dictionary of Medicinal plants. Agrbios pub; 2005: 3, 40, 233, 281, 258, 351.

50. Anonymous. The Unani pharmacopoeia of India. Vol.3 Part 1. New Delhi: GOI Ministry of Health and Family welfare, Dept. of AYUSH; 2007: 50, 62, 88, 107.

51. Najmul Ghani. Khazainul advia. New Delhi: Idara kitabul shifa; YNM: 505-6, 542-3, 853-4, 1208-10, 1248-9.

52. Kabeeruddin. Makhzanul mufradat. 2nd ed. New Delhi: Idara kitabul shifa; 2010: 151, 168, 269-70, 375-6, 387-8.

53. Nagendra Singh and Dixit VK. *Asteracantha longifolia* (L.) Nees, Acanthaceae: Chemistry, traditional, medicinal uses and its pharmacological activities-a review. Brazilian Journal of Pharmacognosy 2010;20(5): 812-17.

54. Kshirsagar AD, Ingale KG, Vyawahare NS and Thorve VS. *Hygrophila spinosa*: A comprehensive review. Pharmacogn Rev Jul-Dec 2010; 4(8): 167-71.

55. Abdul Hakeem. Bustanul mufradat. New Delhi: Idara kitabul shifa; 2002:120-1, 185-6, 209, 352-3, 531, 551-2.

56. Atal CK and Kapur BM. Cultivation and Utilization of Medicinal Plants. Jamu-Tawi:

Regional Research Laboratory, CSIR; 1982: 548.

57. Narayan Das Prajapati, Purohit SS, Arun K Sharma and Tarun kumar. A handbook of medicinal plants. Jodhpur: Agrobios; 2009: 5-6, 281-2, 371, 406, 519-20.

58. Nadkarni KM. Indian plants and drugs. New Delhi: Srishti book distributors; 2005: 4-5, 197-8, 267-8, 306-7, 329-30, 399.

59. Patra A, Jha S and Murthy PN. Phytochemical and pharmacological potential of *Hygrophila spinosa* T. anders. Phcog Rev 2009; 3: 330-41.

60. Chauhan NS, Sharma V and Dixit VK. Effect of *Asteracantha longifolia* seeds on sexual behavior of male rats. Nat Prod Res 2009; 1(9):14.

61. Agrawal HSK and Kulkarni KS. Efficacy and Safety of Speman in patients with Oligospermia: An Open Clinical Study. Indian Journal of Clinical Practice 2003; 2(14): 29-31.

62. Muthulingam M. Antidiabetic efficacy of leaf extracts of *Asteracantha longifolia* (Linn) Nees. On alloxan induced diabetics in male albino Wistar rats. Int j pharm biomed Res 2010; 1 (2): 28-34.

63. Patra A, Murthy PN, Jha S and Aher VD. Anthelmintic and antibacterial activities of *Hygrophila spinosa*T Ander. Res J Pharm Tech 2008; 1:531-2.

64. Patra A, Murthy PN, Jha S, Sahu AN and Roy D. Analgesic and anti-motility activities of leaves of *Hygrophilia spinosa* T Anders. Pharmacologyonline 2008; 2:821-8.

65. Pawar RS, Jain AP, Kashaw SK and Singhai AK. Haematopoetic activity of *Asteracantha longifolia* on cyclophosphamide induced bone marrow depression. Indian J Pharm Sci 2006; 3:337- 40.

66. Usha K, Kasturi GM and Hemalatha P. Hepatoprotective effect of *Hygrophila spinosa* and *Cassia occidentalis* on carbon tetrachloride induced liver damage in experimental rats. Indian J Clin Bio 2007; 22:132-5.

67. Ahmed N, Hussain KF, Sarfaraz M, Zaheen M and Ansari H. Preliminary studies on diuretic effect of *Hygrophila auriculata* (Schum) Heine in rats. Int J Health Res 2009; 2(1); 59- 64.

68. Supriya Kumar Bhattacharjee. Hand Book of Medicinal Plant. 4th ed. Jaipur: Pointer pub.; 2004: 9, 186, 245, 292.

69. James Duke A. Hand book of Medicinal herbs. 2nd ed. London: CRC press; 2006: 1, 493, 534, 645

70. William Charles Evans. Treas and Evans Pharamacognosy.15th ed. Elsevier pub; 2008: 21-28, 208-9, 224, 284, 471, 474, 477, 480.

71. Mohammed Abdul Haleem. Mufradate Azizi. New Delhi: CCRUM; 2009:70, 83.

72. Mayank Thakur and Vinod Kumar Dixit. Ameliorative Effect of Fructo-Oligosaccharide Rich Extract of *Orchis latifolia* Linn. on Sexual Dysfunction in Hyperglycemic Male Rats. Sex Disabl 2008; 26(1): 37-46.

73. Jagdale SP, Shimpi S and Chachad D. pharmacological studies of 'salep'. Journal of Herbal Medicine and Toxicology 2009; 3 (1):153-6.

74. Mahesh Shah. A Case Report of Primary Sterility in the Male. Probe 1979; 18 (4): 271-2.

75. Nauman Aziz, Malik Hassan Mehmood, Hasan Salman Siddiqi, Saf-ur-Rehman Mandukhail and Fatima Sadiq and Wajiha Maan et al. Antihypertensive, antidyslipidemic and endothelial modulating activities of *Orchis mascula*. Hypertension Research Nov 2009; 32: 997-1003.

76. Chatterjee Asima and Prakashi SC. The treatise on Indian medicinal plants. vol 4. New Delhi: NISCIR; 2010:31.

77. Gagan Deep Singh, Sukhcharn Siingh, Navdeep Jindal, Amrinder Bawa S and Dharmesh Saxena C. Physico-chemical characteristics and sensory quality of Singhara, An Indian water chestnut under commercial and industrial storage conditions. Afr J of Food Sci Nov2010; 4(11): 693- 702.

78. Anuj Agrahari k, Khaliquzzama Mohd and Sanjaya Panda k. Evaluation of analgesic activity of methanolic extract of *Trapa natans l.var. Bispinosa* roxb. Roots. JCPR 2010; 01: 8- 11.

79. Mohammad Razvy A, Mohammad Faruk O and Mohammad Hoque A. Environment friendly antibacterial activity of water chestnut fruits. Journal of Biodiversity and Enviro Sci 2011; 1(1):26-34.

80. Patel Samir, David Banji, Otilia Banji JF, Patel MM and Shah KK.Scrutinizing the role of aqueous extract of *Trapa bispinosa* as an immunomodulator in experimental animals. Int J Res Pharm Sci 2010; 1(1): 13-19.

81. Prashanto Das K, Sanjib Bhattacharya, Pandey JN and Moulisha Biswas. Antidiabetic Activity of *Trapa natans* Fruit Peel Extract against Streptozotocin Induced Diabetic Rats.Global J of Pharmacol 2011; 5 (3):186-190.

82. Kar DM, Maharana L, Si SC, Kar MK and Sasmal D. Anti ulcer activity of ethanolic extract of fruit of *Trapa bispinosa* Roxb in animals. Scholars Research Library, Der Pharmacia Lettre 2010; 2(2):190-7.

83. Kirtikar KR and Basu BD. Indian Medicinal Plants. Vol.2. Dehradun: International Book Distributors; 1987: 1090.

84. Anonymous. The Wealth of India- A dictionary of Indian Raw Material and Industrial products.Vol. 10. New Delhi: CSIR; 2003: 275-6.

85. Ambikar DB, Harle UN, Khandare RA, BoreVV and Vyawahare NS. Neuroprotective effect of hydroalcoholic extract of dried fruits of *Trapa bispinosa* Roxb on lipofuscinogenesis and fluorescence product in brain of D-galactose induced ageing accelerated mice. Indian Journal of Experimental Biology Apr 2010; 48:378-82.

86. Vyawahare NS and Ambikar DB. Evaluation of neuro-pharmacological activity of hydroalcoholic extract of fruits of *Trapa*

bispinosa in laboratory animals. Int J Pharmacy Pharm Sci 2010; 2 (2):32-5.

87. Anonymous. The Wealth of India. Vol.1-A. New Delhi: CSIR; 2003:40-1.

88. Kabeeruddin M. Ilmul Advia Nafisi. New Delhi: Ejaz publishing House; 2007:176-7, 334-5.

89. Anomymous. Standardisation of single drug of Unani medicine. part-4. New Delhi: CCRUM; 1997: 29-33.

90. Anomymous. Medicinal plants in folklores of Bihar and Orrisa. 1st ed. New Delhi: CCRUM; YNM.

91. Ibnul Qaf. Kitabul Umda fil Jarahat (Urdu translation). Vol.1 New Delhi: CCRUM; YNM: 276, 293.

92. Gazi MI. The finding of antiplaque features in *Acacia arabica* type of chewing gum. J Clin Periodontol 1991; 18(1): 75-7.

93. Trommer H, Neubert RH, The examination of polysaccharides as potential antioxidative compounds for topical administration using a lipid model system. Inter. J. Pharm 2005. 298: 153-163.

94. Clark DT, Gazi MI, Cox SW, Eley BM and Tinsley GF. The effects of *Acacia arabica* gum on the in vitro growth and protease activities of periodontopathic bacteria. Journal of Clinical Periodontology 1993; 20(4):238-43.

95. Wadood A, Wadood N, Shah SA. Effect of *Acacia arabica* and *Caralluma edulis* on blood glucose levels of normal and allaoxan diabetic rabbits. J. Pak. Med. Assoc.1989. 39: 208-12.

96. Chursi S and Voravuthikunchai SP. Detailed studies on *Quercus infectoria* Olivier (nutgalls) as an alternative treatment for methicillin-resistant Staphylococcus aureus infections. J Appl Microbiol 2009; 106(1):89-96.

97. Saini R and Patil SM. Anti-diabetic activity of roots of *Quercus infectoria* Olivier in Alloxan induced diabetic rats.IJPSR 2012; 3(04): 1318-21.

98. Umachigi SP, Jayaveera KN, Ashok Kumar CK, Kumar GS, Vrushabendra swamy BM and Kishore Kumar DV. Studies on Wound Healing Properties of *Quercus infectoria*. Trop J Pharm Res March 2008; 7 (1): 913-19.

99. Ibn Baitar Z. Al Jamul Mufradatul Advia wal Aghzia. vol.4. New Delhi: CCRUM;YNM:346-8.

100. Kaur G, Hamid H, Ali A, Alam MS and Athar M. Anti-inflammatory evaluation of alcoholic extract of galls of *Quercus infectoria*. J Ethnopharmacol 2008; 90(2- 3):285-292.

101. Aivazi AA and Vijayan VA. Larvicidal activity of oak *Quercus infectoria* Oliv. (Fagaceae) gall extracts against Anopheles stephensi Liston. Parasitol Res 2009; 104(6):1289-93.

102. Rastogi RP and Mehrotra BN. Compendium of Indian Medicinal Plants. Vol.2. Lucknow: CDRI; 1999.

103. Kaur G, Athar M and Alam MS. *Quercus infectoria* galls possess antioxidant activity and abrogates oxidative stress-induced functional alterations in murine macrophages. Chem Biol Interact 2008; 171(3): 272-82.

104. Robert Bently. Medicinal plants. Vol.1-4. New Delhi: Asiatic pub.house; 2002: 68, 94, 249.

105. A.B. Ray. Medicinal Properties of plants: Antifungal, Antibacterial, Antiviral activities. 4th ed. Lucknow: International book distributing company; 2004:5, 440, 553.

106. Ibn Sina. Al Qanoon Fit Tib. (Urdu translation by Kantoori GH). vol 2. New Delhi: Idara Kitabus Shifa; 2007:385.

107. Dedoussis GV, Kaliora AC, Psarras S, Chiou A, Mylona A and Nikolaos Papadopoulos G et al. Antiatherogenic effect of *Pistacia lentiscus* via GSH restoration and downregulation of CD36 mRNA expression. Atherosclerosis 2004; 174: 293-303.

108. Angelike Triantafyllou, Alfiya Bikineyeva, Anna Dikalova, Rafal Nazarewicz, Stamatios

Lerakis and Sergey Dikalov.Anti-inflammatory activity of Chios mastic gum is associated with inhibition of TNF-alpha induced oxidative stress. Nutrition Journal 2011; 10 (64) : 1-9.

109. Chryssavgi Gardeli, Papageorgiou Vassiliki, Mallouchos Athanasios, Theodosis Kibouris and Michael Komaitis. Essential oil composition of *Myrtus communis* L. and *Pistacia lentiscus*L: Evaluation of antioxidant capacity of methanolic extracts. Food chemistry Apr 2008; 107(3):1120-30.

110. Farhad Huwez U. Mastic Gum Kills Helicobacter pylori. New England Journal of Medicine Dec 1998; 339(26): 1946.

111. Zouhir Djerrou, Maameri Z, Hamdi-Pacha Y , Serakta M, Riachi F and Djaalab H et al. effect of virgin fatty oil of *pistacia lentiscus* on

experimental burn wounds healing in rabbits. Afr J Trad CAM 2010; 7 (3): 258 -63.

112. Sana Janakat and Hela Al-Merie. Evaluation of hepatoprotective effect of *Pistacia lentiscus, Phillyrea latifolia* and *Nicotiana glauca*. Journal of Ethnopharmacology 2002; 83: 135-38.

113. Kabiruddin M. Al Qarabadeen. 2nd ed. New Delhi: CCRUM; 2006: 561.

114. Eskenazi B, Wyrobek AJ, Sloter E, Kidd SA, Moore L, Young S and Moore D. The association of age and semen quality in healthy men. Human Reproduction 2003; 18(2):447-54.

115. Bostofte E, Serup J, Bischoff N, Rebbe H. Socio-economic status and fertility of couples examined for infertility, social status and fertility. Andrologia Nov-Dec 1985; 17(6):564-9.

116. Joo KJ, Kwon YW, Myung SC and Kim TH. The Effects of Smoking and Alcohol Intake on Sperm Quality: Light and Transmission Electron Microscopy Findings. J of Int Med Res 2012; 40: 2327 -35.

117. Karagounis CS, Papanikolaou NA, Zavos PM. Semen parameters compared between smoking and non-smoking men: Smoking intensity and semen parameters1985; 8: 373.

118. Vogt HJ, Heleer WD, Borelli S. Sperm quality of healthy smokers, ex-smokers and never smokers. Fertil Steril 1986; 45: 106.

119. Faisal Zakai, Shahab Uddin, Akram M, Mohiuddin E, Abdul Hannan and Khan Usmanghani. Introduction to male infertility. Journal of Medicinal Plants Research Nov 2011; 5(25):5936-45.

120. Tikkiwal M, Ajmera RL, Mathur NK. Effect of zinc administration on seminal zinc and fertility of oligospermic males. Indian J Physiol Pharmacol Jan-Mar1987; 31(1): 30-4.

121. Wong WY, Merkus HM, Thomas CM, Menkveld R, Zielhuis GA, Steegers-Theunissen RP. Effects of folic acid and zinc sulfate on male factor subfertility: a double-blind, randomized, placebo-controlled trial. Fertil Steril Mar 2002; 77 (3): 491-8.

122. Carmely A, Meirow D, Peretz A, Albeck M, Bartoov B,and Sredni B. Protective effect of the immunomodulator AS101 against cyclophosphamide-induced testicular damage in mice. Human Reproduction 2009; 24(6): 1322-9.

123. Amrit Kaur Bansal, Gurmail Singh Bilaspuri. Antioxidant effect of vitamin E on motilityviability and lipid peroxidation of cattle under oxidative stress. Animal Science Papers and Reports 2009; 27 (1):5-14.

124. Jean Parinaud, Dominique Le Lannou, Gerard Vieitez, Jeans Francois Grveau, Pierrette Milhet and Gerard Richoilley. Enhancement of motility by treating spermatozoa with an antioxidant solution (Sperm-fit) following ejaculation. Human Reproduction 1997; 12 (11): 2434-36.

125. Tripathi KD. Essentials of medical pharmacology. 6th ed. New Delhi: Jaypee publishers; 2006: 291, 304-305.